# J. C.
# WATTS

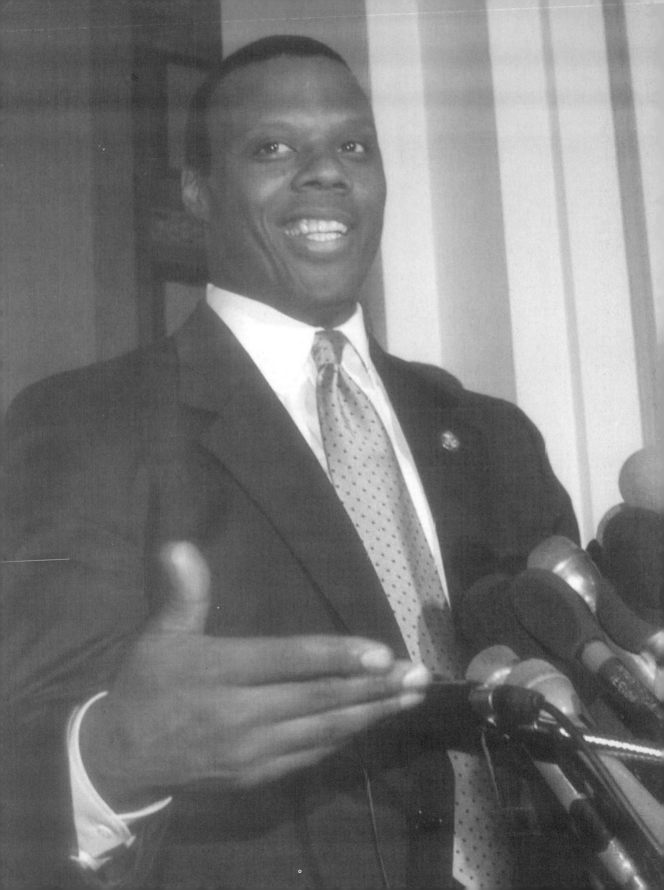

# J. C. WATTS

Norma Jean Lutz

CHELSEA HOUSE PUBLISHERS
*Philadelphia*

**Chelsea House Publishers**

| | |
|---|---|
| *Editor in Chief* | Stephen Reginald |
| *Production Manager* | Pamela Loos |
| *Art Director* | Sara Davis |
| *Director of Photography* | Judy L. Hasday |
| *Managing Editor* | James D. Gallagher |

**Staff for J. C. WATTS**

| | |
|---|---|
| *Associate Art Director* | Takeshi Takahashi |
| *Picture Researcher* | Patricia Burns |
| *Cover Designer* | Keith Trego |

Cover Photo: Corbis/© Alan Levenson

The Chelsea House World Wide Web address is
http://www.chelseahouse.com

First Printing

1 3 5 7 9 8 6 4 2

Lutz, Norma Jean
   J.C. Watts / by Norma Jean Lutz.
   p. cm. — (Black Americans of achievement)
Includes bibliographical references and index.
Summary: Follows the life of J.C. Watts, who played professional
football, served as a Baptist minister, and became the first Republcan
African-American to be elected to Congress from Oklahoma.
ISBN 0-7910-5338-5
      0-7910-5339-3 (pbk.)
1. Watts, J.C. (Julius Caesar), 1957–   Juvenile literature. 2. Afro-
Amercan legislators—United States Biography Juvenile literature.
3. Legislators—United States Biography Juvenile literature.
4. United States. Congress. House Biography Juvenile literature.
5. Afro-Americans—Politics and government Juvenile literature.
[1. Watts, J.C. (Julius Caesar), 1957–   . 2. Legislators. 3. Afro-
Americans Biography.]  I. Title.  II. Series.
E840.8.W39L88 1999
976.6'00496073'0092—dc21                    99-30709
[B]                                          CIP

*For 20 years J. C. Watts has made a name for himself, first as a college football star and later as a Republican congressman from Oklahoma.*

# CONTENTS

# BLACK AMERICANS OF ACHIEVEMENT

HENRY AARON
*baseball great*

KAREEM ABDUL-JABBAR
*basketball great*

MUHAMMAD ALI
*heavyweight champion*

RICHARD ALLEN
*religious leader and social activist*

MAYA ANGELOU
*author*

LOUIS ARMSTRONG
*musician*

ARTHUR ASHE
*tennis great*

JOSEPHINE BAKER
*entertainer*

JAMES BALDWIN
*author*

TYRA BANKS
*model*

BENJAMIN BANNEKER
*scientist and mathematician*

COUNT BASIE
*bandleader and composer*

ANGELA BASSETT
*actress*

ROMARE BEARDEN
*artist*

HALLE BERRY
*actress*

MARY MCLEOD BETHUNE
*educator*

GEORGE WASHINGTON
CARVER
*botanist*

JOHNNIE COCHRAN
*lawyer*

SEAN "PUFFY" COMBS
*music producer*

BILL COSBY
*entertainer*

MILES DAVIS
*musician*

FREDERICK DOUGLASS
*abolitionist editor*

CHARLES DREW
*physician*

W. E. B. DU BOIS
*scholar and activist*

PAUL LAURENCE DUNBAR
*poet*

DUKE ELLINGTON
*bandleader and composer*

RALPH ELLISON
*author*

JULIUS ERVING
*basketball great*

LOUIS FARRAKHAN
*political activist*

ELLA FITZGERALD
*singer*

ARETHA FRANKLIN
*entertainer*

MORGAN FREEMAN
*actor*

MARCUS GARVEY
*black nationalist leader*

JOSH GIBSON
*baseball great*

WHOOPI GOLDBERG
*entertainer*

CUBA GOODING JR.
*actor*

ALEX HALEY
*author*

PRINCE HALL
*social reformer*

JIMI HENDRIX
*musician*

MATTHEW HENSON
*explorer*

GREGORY HINES
*performer*

BILLIE HOLIDAY
*singer*

LENA HORNE
*entertainer*

WHITNEY HOUSTON
*singer and actress*

LANGSTON HUGHES
*poet*

JANET JACKSON
*musician*

JESSE JACKSON
*civil-rights leader and politician*

MICHAEL JACKSON
*entertainer*

| | | | |
|---|---|---|---|
| SAMUEL L. JACKSON
*actor* | JOE LOUIS
*heavyweight champion* | ROSA PARKS
*civil-rights leader* | TINA TURNER
*entertainer* |
| T. D. JAKES
*religious leader* | RONALD MCNAIR
*astronaut* | COLIN POWELL
*military leader* | ALICE WALKER
*author* |
| JACK JOHNSON
*heavyweight champion* | MALCOLM X
*militant black leader* | PAUL ROBESON
*singer and actor* | MADAM C. J. WALKER
*entrepreneur* |
| MAGIC JOHNSON
*basketball great* | BOB MARLEY
*musician* | JACKIE ROBINSON
*baseball great* | BOOKER T. WASHINGTON
*educator* |
| SCOTT JOPLIN
*composer* | THURGOOD MARSHALL
*Supreme Court justice* | CHRIS ROCK
*comedian and actor* | DENZEL WASHINGTON
*actor* |
| BARBARA JORDAN
*politician* | TERRY MCMILLAN
*author* | DIANA ROSS
*entertainer* | J. C. WATTS
*politician* |
| MICHAEL JORDAN
*basketball great* | TONI MORRISON
*author* | WILL SMITH
*actor* | VANESSA WILLIAMS
*singer and actress* |
| CORETTA SCOTT KING
*civil-rights leader* | ELIJAH MUHAMMAD
*religious leader* | WESLEY SNIPES
*actor* | OPRAH WINFREY
*entertainer* |
| MARTIN LUTHER KING, JR.
*civil-rights leader* | EDDIE MURPHY
*entertainer* | CLARENCE THOMAS
*Supreme Court justice* | TIGER WOODS
*golf star* |
| LEWIS LATIMER
*scientist* | JESSE OWENS
*champion athlete* | SOJOURNER TRUTH
*antislavery activist* | RICHARD WRIGHT
*author* |
| SPIKE LEE
*filmmaker* | SATCHEL PAIGE
*baseball great* | HARRIET TUBMAN
*antislavery activist* | |
| CARL LEWIS
*champion athlete* | CHARLIE PARKER
*musician* | NAT TURNER
*slave revolt leader* | |

# ON
# ACHIEVEMENT

❦

*Coretta Scott King*

Before you begin this book, I hope you will ask yourself what the word *excellence* means to you. I think it's a question we should all ask, and keep asking as we grow older and change. Because the truest answer to it should never change. When you think of excellence, perhaps you think of success at work; or of becoming wealthy; or meeting the right person, getting married, and having a good family life.

Those goals are worth striving for, but there is a better way to look at excellence. As Martin Luther King Jr. said in one of his last sermons, "I want you to be first in love. I want you to be first in moral excellence. I want you to be first in generosity. If you want to be important, wonderful. If you want to be great, wonderful. But recognize that he who is greatest among you shall be your servant."

My husband knew that the true meaning of achievement is service. When I met him, in 1952, he was already ordained as a Baptist minister and was working toward a doctoral degree at Boston University. I was studying at the New England Conservatory and dreamed of accomplishments in music. We married a year later, and after I graduated the following year we moved to Montgomery, Alabama. We didn't know it then, but our notions of achievement were about to undergo a dramatic change.

You may have read or heard about what happened next. What began with the boycott of a local bus line grew into a national crusade, and by the time he was assassinated in 1968 my husband had fashioned a black movement powerful enough to shatter forever the practice of racial segregation. What you may not have read about is where he learned to resist injustice without compromising his religious beliefs.

He adopted a strategy of nonviolence from a man of a different race, who lived in a different country and even practiced a different religion. The man was Mahatma Gandhi, the great leader of India, who devoted his life to serving humanity in the spirit of love and nonviolence. It was in these principles that Martin discovered his method for social reform. More than anything else, those two principles were the key to his achievements.

These books are about African Americans who served society through the excellence of their achievements. They form part of the rich history of black men and women in America—a history of stunning accomplishments in every field of human endeavor, from literature and art to science, industry, education, diplomacy, athletics, jurisprudence, even polar exploration.

Not all of the people in this history had the same ideals, but I think you will find that all of them had something in common. Like Martin Luther King Jr., they all decided to become "drum majors" and serve humanity. In that principle—whether it was expressed in books, inventions, or song—they found a goal and a guide outside themselves that showed them a way to serve others instead of living only for themselves.

Reading the stories of these courageous men and women not only helps us discover the principles that we will use to guide our own lives; it also teaches us about our black heritage and about America itself. It is crucial for us to know the heroes and heroines of our history and to realize that the price we paid in our struggle for equality in America was dear. But we must also understand that we have gotten as far as we have partly because America's democratic system and ideals made it possible.

We are still struggling with racism and prejudice. But the great men and women in this series are a tribute to the spirit of the country in which they have flourished. And that makes their stories special and worth knowing.

REPUBLICAN
NATIONAL

# 1

## AMERICA: WHERE DREAMS COME TRUE

❧

*J. C. Watts addresses the delegates at the 1996 Republican National Convention in San Diego. "If a poor black kid from rural Oklahoma can be here tonight," Watts told the crowd, "this great country will allow you to dream your dreams too!"*

EVERY FOUR YEARS in the United States, thousands of members of the two major political parties gather together on separate dates in late summer to choose their party's candidates for president and vice president. Political conventions, as these meetings are called, are noisy affairs complete with banners, streamers, balloons, orchestras, huge projection screens, and all sorts of electronic gadgetry. Amidst the hoopla of the convention, the political party nominates candidates; declares the plans and policies the party's candidate will follow if he or she wins (this is called the party's platform); attempts to unify all areas of the party's membership; and places up-and-coming stars within the party in the spotlight.

Although conventions are not always efficient, they have been part of the American political system for over 150 years. "These confabs long ago stopped choosing presidential candidates, writing serious platforms, and resolving party disputes," John Walcott noted in *U.S. News & World Report* after the 1996 Republican National Convention. "But both the Republican and Democratic conventions survive, like the running of the bulls in Pamplona, or the Apache devil dance, mostly as a ritual link to the past, a means of emptying the wallets of unwary spectators, and an excuse to party."

In August 1996 Republicans from every state in

11

the union converged on San Diego, a coastal city in Southern California. The balloons, streamers, confetti, and projection screens were the same as in years before, but there was little sense of drama as the convention opened. The Republican Party (sometimes called the Grand Old Party, or GOP) had determined its presidential candidate, former senator Robert "Bob" Dole, weeks before. Dole had ensured that he would be nominated by his strong showing in Republican primary elections held in the winter and spring of 1996. Television ratings, the experts said, were down from the convention of 1992.

However those who were still tuned in on the night of Tuesday, August 13, saw a dynamic speaker and rising star in the party. Many were curious about the young congressman from the small town of Eufaula, Oklahoma, who addressed the crowd. Julius Caesar "J. C." Watts Jr. was the only Republican congressman who was African American.

Historically, most blacks have been members of the Democratic Party since the days of Franklin D. Roosevelt. Democrats have typically been seen as the representative of the "working man," supporting the underprivileged through programs such as welfare. The GOP has often been painted as the party of "big business," interested in cutting tax support for welfare and other social programs. More than 90 percent of black voters are registered Democrats. But here was an African American telling the country in clear, confident tones how a Republican presidential administration would benefit all Americans.

"In my wildest imagination," he said, "I never thought that the fifth of six children born to Helen and Buddy Watts—in a poor black neighborhood, in the poor rural community of Eufaula, Oklahoma— would someday be called Congressman.

"But then, this is America . . . where dreams come true."

He went on to tell Americans that character,

which had become an issue in the 1996 presidential race because of the many scandals that dogged incumbent president Bill Clinton, *does* count. "Character," he explained, "is doing what's right when nobody is looking." He defended his party as the one with true compassion, saying, "We don't define compassion by how many people are on welfare . . . or living in public housing. We define compassion by how few people are on welfare . . . and public housing because we have given them the means to climb the ladder of success. . . . I am pleased to tell you that just two weeks ago, the historic Republican Congress passed, over the objections of Bill Clinton, welfare reform that will restore compassion and dignity to those less fortunate.

"Compassion can't be measured in dollars and cents. It does come with a price tag, but that price tag isn't the amount of money spent. The price tag is love, being able to see people as they can be and not as they are. The measure of a man is not how great his faith is, but how great his love is. We must not let government programs disconnect our souls from each other."

Watts summed up his speech by saying, "The American Dream is about becoming the best you can be. . . . If a poor black kid from rural Oklahoma can be here tonight, this great country will allow *you* to dream your dreams too!"

It is a long way from the "wrong side of the tracks" in Eufaula, Oklahoma, to a congressional office in Washington, D.C. The road wasn't always smooth and straight—it took a few twists and turns along the way. How did Julius Caesar Watts Jr. make that journey?

# 2

# DREAMING OF FOOTBALL

EUFAULA, OKLAHOMA, is a small town 82 miles south of Tulsa in the eastern part of the state. The area is both scenic and historic. A landmark called "Standing Rock" marks the place where treaties between the fledgling Confederate States of America and three Native American tribes (Chickasaws, Choctaws, and Creeks) were signed in 1861, just prior to the Civil War.

With its old buildings lining Main Street, the town looks like the set for a western movie. It is near beautiful Eufaula Lake, a man-made reservoir with 600 miles of shoreline. Approximately 3,000 people live in Eufaula today—the same number that lived there when the lake was completed in 1956. A year after the construction of Eufaula Lake was finished, J. C. Watts was born in Eufaula, on November 18, 1957.

The year that J. C. Watts was born, a national controversy erupted in the neighboring state of Arkansas. Nine black students attempted to enter the all-white Central High School in Little Rock, but were prevented when the state's governor, Orval Faubus, ordered the national guard to block the entrances. President Dwight Eisenhower sent in federal troops to face down the guard and the mob, and the students were allowed to enter. This incident marked the beginning of the end of school segregation in America.

*A downtown view of Eufaula, Oklahoma, the small town in which Julius Caesar Watts was born in 1957.*

A few years earlier, one of J. C.'s relatives had been involved in another school segregation case. In the 1940s, a young black woman named Ada Lois Sipuel was denied admission to the University of Oklahoma's law school. She filed a lawsuit against the school and asked the local chapter of the NAACP (National Association for the Advancement of Colored People) for legal assistance. The Reverend Wade Watts, J. C.'s uncle, was president of the Oklahoma chapter of the NAACP and became very involved in the case of *Sipuel v. University of Oklahoma.*

The case went all the way to the Supreme Court, which held that the state was required to provide blacks with equal educational opportunities. In the end the victory was a bittersweet one. Sipuel was required to sit alone in class behind a sign that said "colored" and had to eat behind a chain in the cafeteria so she wouldn't mix with white students. Both of these events, although removed by time and place, would affect the life of young J. C.

By the time J. C. started school, the public schools in Eufaula had been integrated. However the town of Eufaula still seemed to be segregated. It was split in half by railroad tracks. Black families lived on one side of the tracks, whites on the other. J. C. can remember having to sit with other blacks in the balcony of the local movie theater. The blacks were not allowed to sit with the white community in the seats below. After becoming a congressman he commented, "I guarantee there's nobody in the 105th Congress that's been called 'nigger' any more than J. C. Watts."

While his childhood may have been poor, it was by no means rocky. His mother Helen and his father, Julius Caesar "Buddy" Watts Sr., were very present figures in the home, teaching their six children— Melvin, Lawrence, Mildred, Gwendolyn, J. C., and Darlene—the importance of hard work, honesty, and a sense of commitment. The family was close-knit

*Helen and Buddy Watts lived with their family in this ranch house when J. C. was growing up in Eufaula.*

and the siblings watched out for one another.

Outside of Eufaula, Buddy Watts owned 120 to 160 "straggly acres" where he grazed cattle and baled hay. J.C.'s older sister Gwen remembers him driving the hay truck almost before he could reach the pedals. All of the Watts children helped store hay, feed cattle, and raise a big garden.

"My papa always said that the only helping hand you can rely on is at the end of your sleeve," J. C. would say of his father later in life. And Buddy didn't just spout the words, he set the example by working several jobs, which included serving as deputy sheriff during the week and a Baptist pastor on Sundays.

J. C. described the rigorous schedule. "He would work as a cop from 10 P.M. to 7 A.M., come home and sleep two hours, then get up and work from 9:30 to 4:20 or 5, bathe, have dinner and sleep until 9:15, then get up and start again."

J. C.'s uncle, Wade Watts, was a civil rights pioneer in Oklahoma. A former head of the local NAACP chapter, he helped prepare a legal case on behalf of Ada Lois Sipuel, who was seeking admittance to the University of Oklahoma. The case went all the way to the U.S. Supreme Court; the court ordered the university to admit Sipuel. Here, Sipuel is seated next to a university admissions officer, while behind her are (left to right) D. H. Williams of the Oklahoma NAACP, attorney Thurgood Marshall (later a Supreme Court justice himself), and state representative Amos Hall.

Buddy purchased old houses at distress sales, buying them for a low price, fixing them up, and renting them out for $20 or $30 a month. "He did it the hard way," J. C. said of his father. "He did all his own plumbing, carpentry and electrical work—everything." At one point the elder Watts owned more than a dozen houses. "My father would have been embarrassed to take government assistance," J. C. has commented. "That generation was too proud. They made their own way. That generation gave us a foundation of values."

All of the children worked at something almost as soon as they could walk. While other kids could sleep late on Saturdays, the Watts children were required to be up and working, sometimes before daylight. "[My parents] had this thing about work. My sisters had friends who could sleep late on Saturdays. My father wouldn't hear of it. Said it would make them lazy. And my grandmother used to say things like, 'Never marry a woman with long nails. She'll never do a lick of work.'"

Another value that Buddy and Helen Watts taught was respect. "I grew up in a poor part of town," J. C. said, "but we acted civilized, respected adults and knew what was expected of us."

J. C. was introduced to politics at an early age. Both his Uncle Wade and his father were active in politics. Buddy Watts served a stint on the town council in Eufaula, and once ran for police chief. J. C. often tagged along with his uncle when Wade Watts was working for the reelection of Larry Derryberry, a former Oklahoma attorney general.

Derryberry, who later in life would say he considered J. C. Watts one of his best friends, described the young boy tagging along after his Uncle Wade. "I remember he [J. C.] was extremely articulate, very friendly and outgoing."

When J. C. was in the seventh grade, his sister Gwen helped him get a job at J. M.'s Restaurant ("Good Cookin' Since 1955") where she washed dishes. J. C. cleaned up tables, washed dishes, mopped floors, and cleaned up before closing each evening. He worked from 4 to 10 P.M. Monday through Saturday. He wasn't the type of younger sibling who tried to ride on his sister's coattails. He held up his end and did the work cheerfully.

Betty Baily, who still runs J. M.'s Restaurant, remembers giving J. C. his first paycheck at a time when few blacks dared to dine in the restaurant. "He was a good worker, a real good worker," she said. Then referring to his future successes, she added. "I never would have thought of him in that way, didn't see him big in politics."

One of J. C.'s classmates was a girl named Frankie Jones. J. C. liked Frankie, and the feeling was mutual. The two had first met at J. C.'s eighth

*One of J. C.'s first jobs was at J. M.'s Restaurant. The teenager got the job as a busboy through the help of his sister, but he kept it through hard work.*

birthday party, and in sixth grade J. C. had sent her his first love letter.

J. C. thrived in school and became involved in a variety of activities. Although football was his favorite sport, he also played baseball and basketball. Paul Bell, the football coach, had known J. C. since the boy was about two years old. Bell, who spent 19 years coaching the Eufaula Ironheads, was J. C.'s coach when he went out for football as a seventh grader. The coach knew J. C.'s strengths and weaknesses both on and off the field. In junior high school, J. C. played fullback and tailback.

When J. C. was a sophomore in high school, Coach Bell decided to put him at a new position. The team needed someone who could throw the ball, Bell later explained. After the second loss of the season, Bell told his assistant coaches that he was going to put in a young man as quarterback who was willing to work, had a good head, and knew how to lead. He was, of course, referring to J. C. The decision stirred up a minor controversy in Eufaula. A couple of the white team members quit, and a few of the citizens of Eufaula questioned the wisdom of the move—until J. C.'s team started winning games.

"He was just a natural. Just a natural!" Bell says with pride in his voice. "He never disappointed me. Everybody liked and respected J. C. Watts."

In his sophomore year, J. C. became acquainted with the Fellowship of Christian Athletes (FCA), an organization that would have a far-reaching effect on his life for years to come. FCA, headquartered in Kansas City, Missouri, was started in 1954 to give high school athletes the support of Christian fellowship among their peers. Later the organization expanded to include adult athletes as well. At present, the Fellowship of Christian Athletes has more than 350,000 members nationwide.

Chuck Bowman, FCA's director of development in Oklahoma, recalls his first meeting with J. C. Watts. The year was 1973. Bowman was a field representative for FCA at that time, and Watts was a sophomore at Eufaula High School. Bowman says:

> It was early in the morning as I walked into the long, dark hallway of Eufaula High School. As I was standing in the hallway letting my eyes adjust to the darkness I saw this figure walking toward me. It was J. C. Watts and I can still see his electric smile from that morning. . . . He was a sophomore in high school, and from that time on, FCA became a part of his life. FCA became his way of putting his love for sports and his faith together.

Growing up, J. C. never really thought about going to college. For him, the term "getting an education" simply referred to completing high school. He considered joining the Air Force after graduation, because "college wasn't even in our universe," he later said.

But when he was in ninth grade, he happened to see someone he knew while watching a University of

*J. C. Watts began attracting attention to himself on this football field at Eufaula High School. He was the first African American to quarterback the high school team, the Ironheads. Today, a sign at the entrance to the field names Eufaula High's biggest stars, including Lucious Selmon and J. C. Watts.*

Oklahoma football game on television. It was Lucious Selmon, one of three brothers from Eufaula who would become football legends with the Sooners. "I knew him," J. C. said about the incident. "He was from Eufaula. And there he was on national television. I thought that was really neat. So then my idea was to go to college. It had nothing to do with education. It was so I could play football and get on national television like Lucious." From that moment on, he began to work hard on his playing skills.

J. C.'s life changed in 1976 when, during his senior year in high school, he fathered a child. Abortion was never considered, but the girl's parents insisted that she put the baby up for adoption. That was when J. C.'s uncle, the Reverend Wade Watts, stepped into the picture. He and his wife, Betty, adopted the baby and reared her as one of their own. At the time Reverend Watts was pastor at Jerusalem

Baptist Church in McAlester, Oklahoma, and the couple already had 13 children.

The incident was neither covered up nor glossed over. In later years, news reporters who attempted to turn the "revelation" that J. C. Watts had fathered a child out of wedlock into a scandal were unsuccessful. It was old news that everyone already knew. "It was just flat-out dumb," J. C. would later say of the accidental pregnancy. "But those are the times when your faith carries you and you learn from your mistakes. I hope people would give me some credit for taking a bad choice and making the best of it. The child wasn't aborted. The child never received one dime of government assistance. I've been part of her life from day one." His daughter went on to become a straight-A college student.

The turmoil didn't affect his football. In J. C.'s senior year, he was captain of the team and won

*J. C. and his high school basket-ball coach, Perry Anderson, in 1976, the day that the young athlete signed a letter of intent to play football for the University of Oklahoma Sooners.*

nearly every award that mattered to a high school football player. Watts was named Oklahoma Football Player of the Year, selected for the All State Team, and chosen as a high school All-American. Later in the year, he was elected Oklahoma's Athlete of the Year. In addition, his own teammates had elected him captain of his team. It was clear that he'd become serious about his dream to be a star college football player.

"When J. C. stepped into the huddle as quarter-back, he had the attention of everybody," recalled Chuck Bowman. "He had the respect of all the coaches. He was a great student of the game. J. C. had that 'extra gear.' He could be running wide open down the field, slip into another gear and take off from there. His ability as a runner, combined with the ability to throw the ball, gave him an edge."

With this success, it was no surprise that colleges were interested in recruiting J. C. Watts. He would not experience the problems that Ada Lois Sipuel had when she attempted to attend law school in the 1940s. Being a star athlete meant that scouts were speaking with him throughout his senior year, and he had his pick of any number of excellent schools around the nation. "Tulsa University, Oklahoma State University, and the University of Oklahoma were all fighting for him," remembered Coach Bell. "One scholarship offer came from as far away as UCLA."

It's a heady experience for a young person to be so in demand. J. C. weighed the pros and cons of each school, and each athletic program, carefully. The only advice Coach Bell gave him was to hook up with a school that had a winning ball team. "Don't go to a losin' team," Bell told J. C. "They're losin' for a reason, and it's not you!"

In the end, J. C. would choose to remain in Oklahoma. He decided to attend the University of Oklahoma, located in the town of Norman, just south of Oklahoma City. As J. C. Watts left for the large school, he had no way of knowing that one day he would represent the people of the Norman area in the House of Representatives.

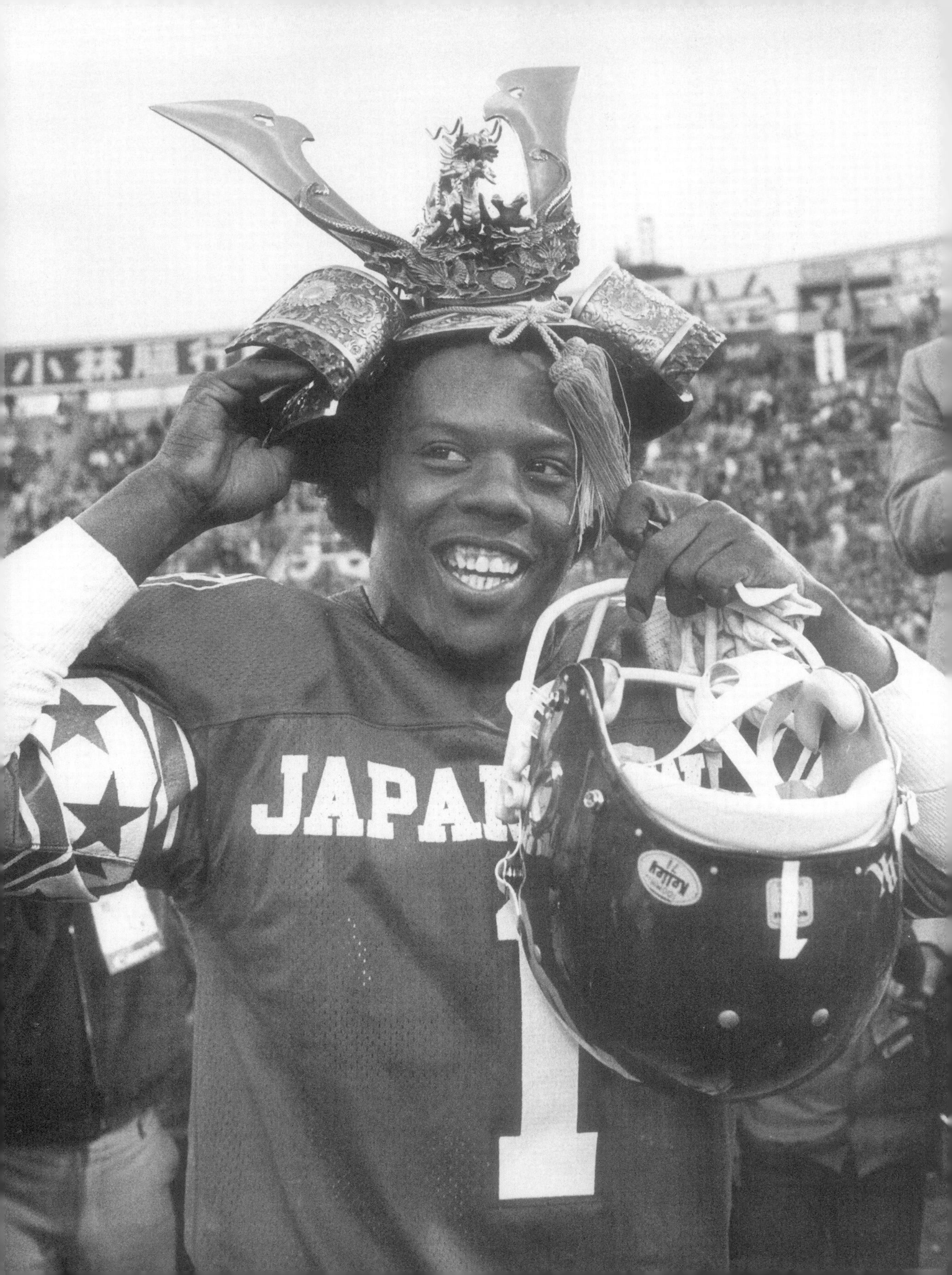
JAPA
1

# 3
## OKLAHOMA UNIVERSITY

*After leading an all-star team of college players to a win in an exhibition game in Japan, J. C. Watts tries on a Samurai warrior's helmet. The game capped off a great college football career for Watts; he started at quarterback and also played as a defensive back in the 25–13 win, and received the Joe Roth Award as the most inspirational player in the game.*

NORMAN, OKLAHOMA, is the third largest city in the state. It had been settled during the Land Rush of 1889, when settlers had been allowed to claim land in the territory. The University of Oklahoma was created by the Oklahoma Territorial Legislature the following year. By the time J. C. arrived on campus in the fall of 1976, the school had 18 colleges and enrolled more than 25,000 students—about eight times the population of Eufaula.

Moving out of the secure cocoon of Eufaula High School, where he'd been a local hero, to the sprawling OU campus was a drastic culture shock for the green freshman. At the university J. C. was a stranger swallowed up in the crowds. Homesick and discouraged, he decided to pack it up and go back home.

When J. C. pulled in the driveway, his father was standing on the porch. When Buddy asked what he was doing, J. C. informed his dad that he had quit. College wasn't for him, he said. But Buddy Watts wouldn't listen. He simply told his son that if college was easy, everyone would be doing it. Then the elder Watts made his son turn around and go right back to school.

During the first few years, however, football seemed to be an elusive dream. Later he would say, "My freshman year I was frustrated and disappointed in not getting to play. Coach [Galen] Hall and Coach

*The campus of the University of Oklahoma was a new world for J. C. Watts when he arrived there in the fall of 1976. Feeling overwhelmed and homesick, he almost quit school, but his father talked him into returning.*

[Barry] Switzer kept saying, 'J. C., be patient. If you stay, you'll play. You've got a future here.'"

But for an ambitious athlete like J. C., it was hard to be patient. He wanted to be out there on Owen Field at Memorial Stadium with the rest of the OU team. To make things worse, he was "redshirted" during his sophomore year. This term refers to a five-year program for students with athletic scholarships. The extra year gives them a chance to catch up on studies, and prevents burnout. However, although the student-athletes can practice with the team in their extra, or "redshirt" year, they are not allowed to play. According to J. C., his sophomore year was like his freshman year all over again.

J. C. Watts had never been a great student. His main objective in high school had been simply to pass. He later admitted that the reason that he studied to get passing grades was that he "couldn't stand the embarrassment of being declared ineligible to play sports." It was not until his redshirt season in college that he decided to stretch himself mentally. He resigned himself to the fact that the good things he expected on the football field were not going to happen overnight, and he threw himself into his studies as a mass communications major in the OU School of Journalism.

Later, J. C. would say that he went to OU to play football, but decided not to major in it. He wanted to come out of school with a good education, not just a series of football honors and trophies for his shelf. The importance of a good education was stressed by the coaches at Oklahoma. "Coach Switzer used to tell us that our academics would take us much farther than our athletic ability," J. C. told *Sooners Illustrated* in 1991.

Lynda Lee Kaid, a professor in the journalism school at that time remembers J. C. as being an articulate and conscientious student. Professor Kaid taught a sports broadcasting course, and J. C. was on the production staff of a weekly show that aired on the cable network. "His charisma came across well on TV," Kaid said about her student. "I've always

*Since J. C. Watts was not making his mark on the football field in his freshman and sophomore years, he attempted to make his mark in the classroom instead. He threw his energy into his communications studies. One professor, Lynda Lee Kaid, later commented, "I've always said I thought he would do well on television, but I certainly never knew it would turn out to be in the area of politics."*

said I thought he would do well on television, but I certainly never knew it would turn out to be in the area of politics."

In spite of the fact that J. C. led an extremely busy life as a student, Kaid attests to the fact that he was a man of his word. "He always did what he said he would do. He had the mark then of what we see in him now." Kaid, who presently teaches Political Communications, occasionally invites Congressman Watts back to the University of Oklahoma to speak to her students.

By now, J. C. had married Frankie, his childhood sweetheart. In 1976 their daughter Lakeisha was born, and son Jarrelle came along in 1979. His growing family made an even greater demand on his time.

The opportunity to play for the OU Sooners came at last in the fall of 1978, two full years after his arrival on campus. The hero of Oklahoma football at that time was Thomas Lott. Lott had been the starting quarterback for OU for three years and was a two-time All-Big Eight Conference selection. But when Lott suffered an ankle injury in the fourth period of a game against Oklahoma's rival, the University of Texas, J. C. Watts was suddenly thrust into the limelight. He led the Sooners into the end zone, throwing a 22-yard pass to set up a touchdown run as Oklahoma won, 31–10.

He was cool afterward, telling *Tulsa Tribune* sports writer Bob Hartzell, "I wasn't nervous at all when they told me to go in."

This first look at J. C. in a pressure situation excited Sooners fans and sports writers. Thomas Lott was scheduled to graduate in the spring of 1979, so many wondered if Watts could replace the Oklahoma star. As the team worked out in the summer of 1979, Oklahoma coach Barry Switzer expressed confidence that J. C., now a junior, could be as good as Thomas Lott had been. A teammate, center Paul Tabor, agreed. "J. C. has been here three years and he is

mature," Tabor told the *Tulsa Tribune*. "Now he has gained confidence, partly because he knows he is No.1. I think he will do well."

J. C. was fortunate to share the backfield with one of the best running backs in the country, Billy Sims. In 1978, as a junior, Sims had won the Heisman Trophy, which is awarded to the nations' best collegiate football player each season. He had rushed for 1,762 yards, averaging more than seven and a half yards per carry, and led the nation in scoring with 20 touchdowns. Sims was only the sixth junior to win in the 44-year history of the Heisman award.

But even though the presence of Billy Sims, who was having another great season as a senior, overshadowed the accomplishments of Oklahoma's young quarterback, Sooners fans soon recognized

*J. C. is overwhelmed by Kansas tacklers in the first start of his college career, on October 14, 1978. Despite this, he led the Sooners to a 17–16 win over Kansas to preserve the team's unbeaten record to that point. J. C. had gotten his opportunity to play a week earlier, when starting quarterback Thomas Lott was injured in a game against Texas. His performance while Lott was recovering excited Oklahoma fans, who anticipated that J. C. could step into the quarterback spot when Lott graduated at the end of the year.*

that J.C. was a fine player in his own right. The team defeated 10 of 11 opponents on their regular schedule, won the Big Eight championship, and received a bid to play in one of the major New Year's Day bowl games, the Orange Bowl, held in Miami. Watts's patience, diligence, and hard work were beginning to pay off.

On New Year's Day 1980, the Sooners found themselves facing hometown favorite Florida State University. In the first 17 minutes FSU took a 7–0 lead. The crowd was wildly cheering for FSU, but Watts soon quieted them with a 61-yard touchdown run. He guided the Sooners to a couple more goals, capping the victory with a fourth-quarter 22-yard pass to Sims for the game's final touchdown. For his important role in Oklahoma's 24–7 victory, J. C. Watts was selected the Orange Bowl's Most Valuable Player.

It had been a great year for the Oklahoma football team. The Sooners finished the year 11–1, and were ranked No. 3 in the nation in the Associated Press's poll. Star running back Billy Sims had again led the nation in scoring, with 22 touchdowns, and had rushed for more than 1,500 yards. In a close vote, he finished second in the balloting for the Heisman Trophy. A few months later, Sims was the first player chosen in the 1980 NFL draft. After graduation, he went on to a professional football career with the Detroit Lions, where he was named Rookie of the Year in his first season, was named to the Pro Bowl three times, and set team records for single-season and career rushing yardage before a 1984 knee injury ended his playing days prematurely.

As the 1979 Sooners had been Billy Sims's team, so the 1980 squad would depend on J. C. Watts to lead them to victory. By the summer of 1980, J. C. had experienced his first taste of being a star. Word of his excellent speaking abilities had spread, bringing him more invitations to speak than he could possibly handle. And he was recognized on sight. "It's rare that he can walk into a store, a business office, or even a crowded movie theater anywhere in Oklahoma that he is not recognized," wrote *Daily Oklahoman* columnist Jim Lassiter.

To understand this kind of fame, one must understand how important football is in Oklahoma. Some have referred to it as a "second religion." Games against Oklahoma State University, Nebraska, and Texas are the most important to loyal Sooners fans. Fans are serious, and they are fickle. They are as quick to boo as they are to cheer.

In the early weeks of his senior year, J. C. was to hear a few of those boos. The team lost tough games to Stanford and Texas, the latter by a 20–13 score. Watts shouldered a lot of the blame for the loss to Oklahoma's rival because he had fumbled three times and thrown four interceptions. "There's no doubt that was the worst football game I've played in my football career, not only college but also high school," he admitted later. "I *never* played that bad. It was a depressing time. I didn't get very much sleep. I did a lot of praying about it. It all worked out. I knew any time you've got a low point, there's gonna be high points. . . . I just went out and told myself, 'Hey don't get down on yourself; you've got seven games left and you can turn this thing around and have a heckuva season.' That's exactly what we did."

While fans were booing and criticizing Watts and the coaches, Switzer defended his quarterback. "J. C. Watts is our best quarterback. He's our best passer and we were behind in the game and we needed his abilities in there." The two men have remained lifelong friends. In later years, when a former Oklahoma linebacker named Brian Bosworth wrote a book accusing Switzer and the OU team members of problems with drugs and cheating on tests, J. C. came to his coach's defense both in his speeches and in print.

All during his senior year at OU, J. C. kept an exclusive taped diary of his feelings before each

Sooner game. He felt as star quarterback, it was his duty to "satisfy the fans on and off the field. The fans are a big part of our success," he said. "And I think it's important to us to show them we care." This ability to give freely of himself would surface many times in the future in his ministry, his family life, and his political life.

The diary reflects his excitement as the team pulled together after the disappointing Texas loss. The Sooners reeled off eight straight victories, including a 21–17 win over rival Nebraska in November 1979. This victory sealed the Big Eight title for the second year, and once again the Sooners were invited to the Orange Bowl. After the pivotal victory over the Cornhuskers, Watts commented in his diary, "Friends, a month ago if you had told me we might be going to the Orange Bowl to play for the national championship, I'd have asked you if you had a good dentist, because I'd have fought you for telling me something that foolish."

But it was true. The Sooners would again be in Florida on New Year's Day. Once again they would face a tough Florida State team; the Gators, coached by Bobby Bowden, were ranked in the top five by the Associated Press and brought a 10–1 record into the game. Oklahoma, meanwhile had finished the season 9–2.

The 1981 Orange Bowl turned out to be a nail-biting, edge-of-your-seat game. With 3:19 remaining in the fourth quarter, Florida State held a 17–10 lead. It was up to J. C. Watts to lead the team into the end zone. He brought the Sooners down the field, completing an 11-yard touchdown pass to Steve Rhodes with 1:27 left and bringing the team within one point, 17–16. Oklahoma could have tied the game by kicking the extra point, but Watts and coach Switzer decided to go for the win by attempting a two-point conversion. When the ball was snapped, J. C. scanned the field, then threw a strike to tight end

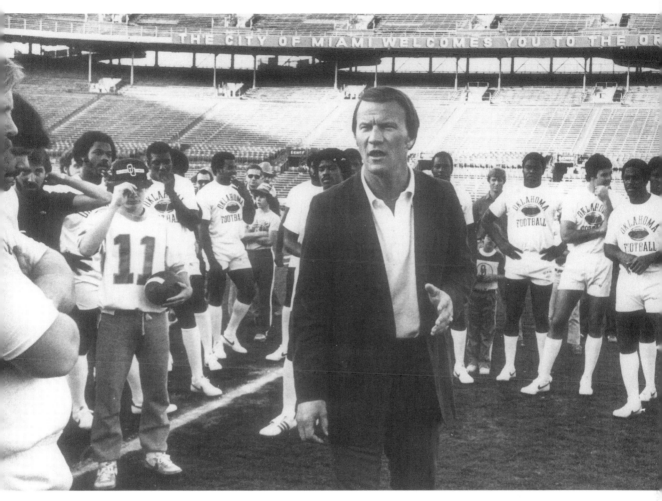

Forest Valora. The Sooners were leading, 18–17, and there was no way Oklahoma's defense was going to let Florida score.

The Orange Bowl victory capped off a great season, and career, for J. C. Watts. For the second year in a row, he was voted the game's Most Valuable Player. In the regular season, he had finished second in the nation in scoring with 18 touchdowns. With J. C. directing the offense, Oklahoma finished the year with a 10-2 record and was ranked third in the nation once again. During his two years as Oklahoma's starting quarterback, Watts compiled a 22–3 career record, including a perfect 15–0 record in the Big Eight

*Oklahoma's head coach, Barry Switzer, addresses the squad during a practice session before the 1981 Orange Bowl. Switzer was a highly regarded team motivator who had turned the Sooners into a national powerhouse.*

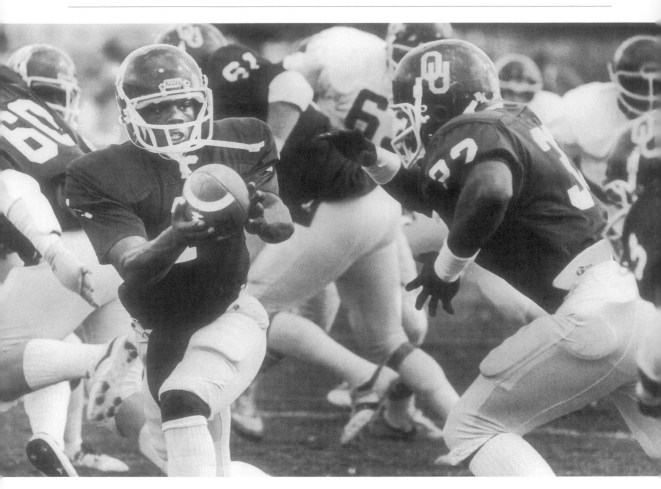

*J. C. hands off during a team practice before the 1981 Orange Bowl. Watts and the Sooners overcame a bad start to the season to earn another bid to the prestigious game, then came from behind to beat Florida State, 18–17*

Conference and two conference championships.

Two weeks after the exhilarating Orange Bowl victory, J. C. flew to Japan, where he played in the East-West Bowl on January 18, 1981. J. C. played both offensive and defensive roles in the Yokohama all-star game, in which the best college players showcase their talents. He was selected as the game's most inspirational player. Back home in Eufaula, the town council decided to rename the two-block street on which J. C. lived. The sign that had said "Andrew Jackson Street" was taken down, and a new one that read "J. C. Watts Street" was put up in its place. The hometown boy had made good.

In his taped diary, J. C. said this about the season:

There were times early in the season when I could have quit. But when my teammates elected me as one of their captains, they did so because they believed in me. And I was expected to keep my head up even when thing got tough. I had to fight back. I had to be strong.

At Oklahoma University, J. C. learned to take the bitter with the sweet, to think on his feet, and to stay calm under fire. All of those attributes would be vital in the days that lay just ahead.

# 4

## LESSONS FROM FOOTBALL

"*I've got to start a career in something else, and hopefully professional football. If not, I'll get on with some independent oil company. I've thought about politics. . . . Someday I'd like to run for Senate or governor or something like that.*"

—J. C. Watts, message in his taped diary,
March 1981.

On the move, Watts fires a pass to an Ottawa teammate in a Canadian Football League game. Although he was disappointed not to be drafted as a quarterback by an NFL team, J. C. fashioned a five-year career as a signal-caller north of the border.

Television cameras, bright lights, microphones, and roving reporters crowded into the Sheraton Hotel in New York City. It was April 1981, and the media was on hand to report the signing of players for the NFL draft. The first pick of the draft, Heisman Trophy–winning running back George Rogers, and selections of the best college players through early rounds were hot news. By the eighth round of the draft, however, the cameras were gone and the lights were no longer shining. This was when the New York Jets picked J. C. Watts.

For the young athlete, the selection was disappointing. He had expected to be picked by at least the sixth round. Also, the Jets drafted him to play defensive back. J. C. Watts wanted to be a quarterback. "I guess it would have been a lot easier on me," he said, "if I hadn't gotten drafted at all."

While he admitted that playing professional football had been his dream, he still remained

*In his first season in the CFL, J. C. had an immediate impact. He turned a losing Ottawa team around, leading the squad to the championship game, the Grey Cup, and being named the game's Most Valuable Player despite a 26-23 loss to Edmonton.*

open-minded. He had seen that many of his former teammates, even the better players, had not always been drafted in the NFL. "If it doesn't happen for me, I'm not going to fight it. There probably wouldn't be a better time to say goodbye than right now," he told the *Daily Oklahoman.* "I can get out now with my head up. Now would be the time to do it."

After his first training session with the Jets, J. C. knew that he might never take a snap as an NFL quarterback. But there was another option that would allow him to play professionally at the quarterback position: the Canadian Football League (CFL). The CFL was not as well-known as its American counterpart, but some college stars did opt to play professionally north of the border, and the Ottawa Rough Riders had offered J. C. a contract to play quarterback.

The team derived its nickname "Rough Riders"

from the Canadian lumberjacks who rode down the rapids of the Ottawa River in the frontier days. The Rough Riders team played its first game in 1867, against the Senators. It was not until 1883 that the Ontario Rugby Football Union was formed. At that time the playing squads were composed of 15 men, but by 1905 the number was finally reduced to 12. In 1909 Lord Earl Grey, the governor general of Canada, donated a trophy to be awarded to the champions of the Canadian Rugby Football Union. Each year since, the best professional teams in Canada have vied for the "Grey Cup." The famed Grey Cup is comparable to the Super Bowl in the United States.

J. C. was interested in the CFL and signed a contract with the Rough Riders. The young quarterback participated in workouts with the team over Memorial Day weekend 1981. He stayed at Trent University in Peterborough, in a dormitory at a beautiful campus that featured wildlife sanctuaries, maple-beech forests, and meadow wetlands. But the confused J. C. wasn't looking at the trees or listening to the bird calls. He felt confused and uncertain. "I'm out in the middle of nowhere—at least what I thought was the middle of nowhere," he recalled. "It was brutal."

J. C. participated in two workouts with the Rough Riders on Sunday. But on Monday, he told head coach George Brancato that he was leaving. Back in Oklahoma there was a public relations job waiting for J. C. with the King Energy Company in Oklahoma City, and that seemed to be the right thing to do. Watts hopped a plane back to Oklahoma. "I don't think I'd be fair to my teammates, to the staff and management because my heart's just not in it," Watts told a reporter for the *Norman Transcript*.

"He didn't want to play football anymore," Rough Rider public relations director Bill Houldsworth explained to the *OKC Times*. "He'd had a few sleepless nights. . . . and a lot of things had been gnawing at him: what does he do? Does he come to Canada to play football, does he sign with the Jets, or does he take the business opportunity? That's a tough decision for a 23-year-old."

The Rough Riders, however, kept the door in Canada wide open. Houldsworth said, "Our general manager told [J. C. Watts] if he does change his mind to call us."

It took about six weeks, but J. C. did change his mind. Ottawa's season had gotten off to a shaky start as the squad had lost its first two games. The team's two quarterbacks, both from the United States, were having trouble adjusting to the Canadian game. In the CFL the field is 20 yards longer and 10 yards wider than the field in the NFL. Canadian football is more of a wide-open game, and everyone is on the run as soon as the ball snaps.

The Ottawa club had been in contact with Watts's agent, Abdul Jalil of San Francisco, trying to get Watts to return to the Rough Riders. Finally, an agreement was reached. J. C. shed his business suit, packed up his family, moved north to Ottawa, and joined the team.

By the time Watts arrived in Ottawa, it was already late in the season. His first game was on October 12 against the Edmonton Eskimos. Although the Eskimos came out on top, 24–6, Watts had completed 29 of 51 passes for 338 yards.

J. C. improved and so did the team. With J. C. at quarterback for the last five games of the season, the Rough Riders won 3 and lost 2. Ottawa entered the playoffs with just a 5–11 record but won its first two playoff games—including a surprising 17–13 upset of the Hamilton Tiger-Cats in which Watts passed for 311 yards and ran for another 46. That win spoiled the 11–4–1 Tiger-Cats' hope of reaching the finals of the Grey Cup. Hamilton's coach Frank Kush knew why they lost. "Defensively, we couldn't stop Watts," he said after the game. "He did a great job of scrambling, doing what he's good at."

The victory meant the Rough Riders would go to Montreal for their first Grey Cup appearance since 1976. Snapping up the Grey Cup, however, wouldn't be easy. Their opponents, the Edmonton Eskimos, had made eight trips to the Grey Cup finals in nine years, and had become the first team in CFL history to win four consecutive Grey Cup games. Few teams had been able to challenge the Eskimos, who had racked up a 14–1–1 record in the regular season. Edmonton was favored by more than three touchdowns over the Rough Riders, who had the worst record of any team that had ever played for the Grey Cup.

The game started off with a strong surge by the Rough Riders that shocked the Eskimos. After the opening kickoff, Watts directed the team to the Edmonton 27 yard line, where Gerry Organ kicked a field goal. By halftime, Ottawa was leading 20 to 1. (In CFL scoring, a kick through the end zone is worth one point.)

In the second half, the Eskimos seemed to shake out of their stupor. They roared back to tie the game with just over 10 minutes left in the fourth quarter. Then with three seconds left, their kicker Dave Cutler made a 27-yard field goal to give Edmonton the victory, and the Grey Cup, 26–23. The *Daily Oklahoman* referred to the Rough Riders' game as a "gutsy performance." J. C. compared the disappointing defeat with losing to Texas when he was a senior at Oklahoma.

Even though the Rough Riders lost, Watts had proven he could be a star in the CFL. He was named the game's Most Valuable Player. The Canadian fans took to him immediately. But by the spring of 1982, his relationship with the team management had soured. A major disagreement arose over how J. C.'s salary was being paid.

"I was under the impression when I negotiated my contract that I would be paid in U.S. funds," Watts said. Instead he was paid in Canadian dollars, which at that time were worth about 80 cents on the U.S. dollar, making his income much less—about $8,500 less. "I tried to get this straight all year," he added. "We argued through to Grey Cup week and it was never settled."

Watts went back to Oklahoma, prepared to sit out the next season. By this time he was a partner in an eastern Oklahoma oil company, a business that was just getting off the ground. (He'd named the company the Ironhead Petroleum Company after his high school team, the Eufaula Ironheads.) In addition he volunteered much of his time to the Fellowship of Christian Athletes, and because of his OU fame was a much-sought-after banquet speaker. And with a growing family, he didn't lack things to do.

There was yet another thought in the back of J. C.'s mind. He still wished he could have a chance at a quarterback job in the NFL. "I'd like to see if I could play there," he said. "I've always had confidence in my mental game and the NFL scouts told me at the time of the draft they knew I had a strong arm." This was one dream, however, that was never to be. At five feet 11 inches and 190 pounds, Watts was thought by most NFL scouts to be too small to play quarterback in the National Football League, and he was never given an opportunity.

J. C. did indeed sit out the 1982 season. In August 1983, with a new contract, the former OU quarterback returned to thrill the crowds in Ottawa. He played two more successful seasons with the Rough Riders, then signed a contract with the Toronto Argonauts for the 1986 season.

At the end of that year J. C. felt it was time to leave football. He told his wife Frankie that he had played his last professional football game. Surprised, she asked him what he was going to do next. He answered, "I don't know. I just think the Lord is speaking to my heart to move on."

The season in J. C.'s life for football was over, but

he would continue to use the lessons he learned from the game. J. C. would later comment:

> Football has taught me about myself, and what it takes to go through life—hard work, discipline, teamwork, delayed gratification, character, and getting up when you're down. It was also one of my first experiences of "crossing the tracks." In football I could rely on my talents and will alone. My coaches didn't care if I was black, red, or green, and so it reinforced my faith that if a black man from Eufaula, Oklahoma could make it with a strong will, anyone else could too.

*"Football has taught me about myself, and what it takes to go through life," J. C. Watts once commented. After four seasons with Ottawa and another with the Toronto Argonauts, he decided to retire from the game after the 1986 season.*

# 5

## YEARS AT SUNNYLANE

❦

SINCE THE EARLY 1900s, Oklahoma has been famous for its oil and petroleum industries. The city of Tulsa especially had become an important center of the nation's petroleum business, with large refineries and plants that produced petroleum products. Several major oil companies had their corporate offices and research laboratories there. Tulsa was aptly nick-named the Oil Capital of the World. However there was a downside: the state relied so completely on one major source of revenue that problems in that indus-try would reverberate throughout the state.

During the 1970s oil prices had risen dramati-cally, giving speculators a false sense of security. Then prices plunged in the early 1980s—just as J. C. Watts was becoming more deeply involved in the petroleum industry. This period of time in the state's history is now referred to as the "Oil Bust."

"When I first started my own oil business . . . I thought I was getting in at a good time," Watts told the *Tulsa Tribune* in 1982. "But after three months, business started slowing down. I might end up being the most broke oil man in town."

The 1980s would be a decade of financial difficul-ties for J. C. Watts. At one point he purchased some property in Cleveland County, Oklahoma. He wanted to drill for oil on the land, which was originally val-ued at $104,000. However, with the Oil Bust, the

*Tulsa was a major center of the oil industry in the 1970s and 1980s; after J. C. Watts ended his pro football career, he began to immerse himself more deeply into his petroleum business in Oklahoma. Unfortunately, this coincided with a downturn in the oil market, and J. C. soon found himself in financial trouble.*

*The Reverend John Lucas of Sunnylane Baptist Church became a friend and mentor to J. C. after he retired from football.*

value of this land tumbled along with oil prices. When Watts was unable to pay his mortgage on the property, Security National Bank in Norman foreclosed and sold the tract. Watts still owed $46,000 to the bank, but now he did not own the land. This debt would pose problems for him in the future, because when Security Bank changed ownership, it would refile its claim for the money he owed. Future political opponents would try to use this against J. C. by asserting that he had a number of bank claims against him.

In fact, it was just the one debt.

During the early '80s, J. C. also tried his hand at promoting professional boxing in the Oklahoma City area. The organization he put together was called Top Contenders. However, this venture was short-lived.

While he played football for the Canadian Football League, J. C.'s seemingly high wages had been eroded by having to pay taxes in both the United States and Canada. In addition, the CFL had agreed to pay Watts's taxes in Oklahoma, but this had not been done. It was a rude awakening for J. C. to learn that he owed back taxes in his home state. Eventually three tax liens would be filed against him. Diligently he made the payments required of him.

Worse yet was the matter of medical insurance. When Frankie became seriously ill, J. C. learned that the medical insurance promised by the CFL was nonexistent. This put him in debt to a local hospital for over $2,000. J. C. paid the amount.

Close friends at this time advised him to file bankruptcy. After all, it would certainly be understandable and forgivable under such adverse circumstances. But J. C. refused. Doing what was right was more important. And paying what he owed, he felt, was the right thing to do.

Frankie Watts gave birth to the couple's third child, a daughter they named Jennifer, in 1985. With a growing family, a failing business, and financial problems, the usually optimistic J. C. Watts felt that he was at a crossroads in his life.

From the time J. C. had been a football star at the University of Oklahoma, he had been asked to speak to various groups and organizations all across Oklahoma. One place he had visited was Sunnylane Southern Baptist Church in Del City, a suburb of Oklahoma City. The church is situated in an industrial area near Tinker Air Force Base and the General Motors Plant—the two largest employers in the area. Sunnylane Baptist's congregation was made up of blue-collar whites.

The pastor, John Lucas, was a warm-hearted man who took a real liking to J. C. Watts. While J. C. was visiting the church, a photo was taken of the two of them together. This photo was then hung on the wall of the pastor's office.

Brother John, as the pastor was called by his parishioners, loved the youth of his church. He enjoyed joking and teasing and having fun with them. Never stuffy or aloof, Brother John would even go to Falls Creek Camp with his kids each summer where, as one church member recalled, "His fun-loving pranks and jokes got the kids in more trouble than the kids got into themselves."

However, no matter how much Brother John loved the kids, his pastoral duties kept him from doing all that he wanted to do with them. What he really needed was a full-time youth pastor. As he prayed about this need, he kept feeling his attention turn to the photo of J. C. on his office wall. It seemed like such a long shot to ask such a busy, well-known personality to join the staff at his small church. The salary certainly wouldn't be much.

John's wife, Helen, confesses that when John first told her of his plan to invite J. C. Watts to be their youth pastor, she was not totally in favor. "John," she told him, "if you have J. C. Watts come to Sunnylane, everyone will leave." The year was 1987 and there was still plenty of prejudice in their part of the country.

In spite of what his wife said, Rev. John Lucas couldn't get J. C. off his mind. At last he called and invited the former OU football star to become the youth pastor at Sunnylane Baptist.

About that time, J. C. was looking at a number of options. He'd just been offered a coaching position at Baylor University in Texas, the largest Baptist University in the country. However, after thinking and praying about Lucas's offer, J. C. definitely felt that working with the children of Sunnylane was something God wanted him to do. While he'd been speaking to hundreds of young people at various events sponsored by the Fellowship of Christian Athletes, here was an opportunity to affect young lives on a more personal, one-to-one basis.

After J. C. agreed to join the church's staff, the congregation still had to vote on the matter. They voted in favor, and contrary to Helen Lucas's prediction no one left the church. In this particular instance, she was glad to be wrong. "I came to have a high regard for J. C.," she said, then added, "Everyone in our church did! J. C. was special, and he was genuine."

The Reverend John Lucas came to love J. C. like a son. "J. C. and John spent hours together and had many long heart-to-heart talks," Helen recalled. Those conversations drew J. C. into a closer walk with God. On December 11, 1988, a visiting speaker came to Sunnylane to hold a series of special meetings. The messages were focused on salvation in Christ. J. C. recalls that the preacher said, "If you are 99 percent sure [about salvation], then you are 100 percent lost." As a young boy of seven, J. C. had walked down a church aisle and asked to be baptized, but he still felt he wasn't 100 percent sure.

"So on December 11, as a youth minister, I asked Christ to come into my heart and be my personal Savior. I squared it away at that time," J. C. explained. As a 31-year-old, J. C. Watts was again baptized in water, this time by his pastor John Lucas.

*As the youth leader of Sunnylane Baptist Church, J. C. was involved in many activities— including this Christmas program in which he appeared as Santa Claus. With him at the microphone is John Lucas.*

Following this decision, J. C.'s Christian commitment became stronger and more sure than ever before.

Sunnylane's youth group thrived under J. C.'s leadership. "He did everything with us," remembers one of the young people in the church who came under J. C.'s leadership for seven years. "J. C. was like one of the kids, and yet he held a firm hand of authority."

As youth pastor, J. C. expected the kids to follow rules, pay attention, and respect authority. Nelda Valdez Lee appreciated that about J. C. "He demonstrated to the kids how to get under authority and how to respect that authority," she said. "He never bucked the pastor, or complained about how the church was being run."

Nelda was one of the Sunday school teachers when J. C. came on as the youth pastor. In the ensuing years, as her two children came into the youth department, she became like a "right hand" to J. C., not only teaching but also helping at youth functions and serving as a leader at Falls Creek summer camp. In that position she saw J. C. in many different situations and under a variety of circumstances. However she remembers J. C. as being a consistent "man of character and integrity. He's a man," she added, "who seeks the Lord in just about everything he does."

"He taught our kids by example," Nelda explained. "He showed by example what a father should be. He cared for his family and showed love and respect to his wife. And he was always quick to say 'I forgive,' or 'I was wrong' whenever the situation called for it."

Kids who had never come to church before began attending church on Wednesday nights, and the youth group grew. "His focus was not on recreation," commented Jerry Don Abernathy, who became pastor of Sunnylane in 1990, "but he knew how to have good clean fun. The kids loved him."

On one occasion J. C. brought in a few guys from

the Sooners football squad. Here were some of the big Oklahoma superstars, and J. C. had them play an exhibition *basketball* game in the church gym. One spectator, Nicole (Valdez) Alston, remembers having plenty of popcorn and getting autographs from the football heroes. "It was funny and fun," she said, "to see the football players playing a game of basketball."

"He captured their attention with fun things," Abernathy pointed out, "then he preached a strong message that challenged them to live their lives for the Lord."

Abernathy recalled a time when J. C. learned that one of the youths in the group had been drinking. For that Sunday night lesson, J. C. presented to the kids a beaker of water and a beaker of alcohol. To show them the effects of alcohol, he dropped a worm in the water and the worm kept swimming. Then he dropped a worm in the alcohol and it immediately died. He took the time to teach creatively, and to address issues, rather than spouting words.

In 1996 when Congressman J. C. Watts spoke to the nation about the subject of character, it was nothing new to the youth at Sunnylane. They had heard that message many times before. "He always told us," Nicole said, "that character meant doing what was right when no one was looking."

The other message the Sunnylane youth group members would remember was "stay focused." Learning to stay focused was a principle J. C. had learned out on the football field when there were only two minutes to play and the score was tight. "Stay focused," he'd tell the kids, "and don't let the things of the world distract you from the things of God."

By July of 1990, J. C. had settled in at Sunnylane. Then tragedy struck. His friend John Lucas died during surgery. Brother John's death was a shock to everyone who knew him. At the funeral, J. C. told the grieving crowd that John Lucas had made a greater impact on his life than any person other than

FALLS CREEK 1990

*The youth group of Sunnylane Baptist church, in a photo taken in July 1990 at the Falls Creek camp. Reverend John Lucas and J. C. Watts are in the top row at the left. The picture was taken just a few days before Lucas died suddenly during surgery.*

his own father. With John's passing, J. C. had lost a pastor, mentor, friend, and father figure.

But things had to move forward, and another pastor was now needed. It would be tough for the new church leader to follow in the footsteps of Sunnylane's beloved John Lucas. Jerry Don Abernathy became the pastor following Lucas's death. "And it was J. C. who help me and the others make the difficult adjustment," Sunday school teacher Nelda explained. "I watched J. C. remain under the pastor's authority no matter what changes had to be made. J. C. kept his strength and character consistent through that time. It helped the youth," she said, "but it helped me personally as well."

Jerry Don Abernathy had known J. C. from the

times when the Reverend had conducted revivals at Sunnylane, so the two were not strangers. Upon their arrival at Sunnylane, Anne Abernathy, Jerry Don's wife, happened to be standing in J. C.'s office. She admired a particular picture he had hanging on his wall. "You like it?" J. C. asked her. When she assured him she did, he said, "I'll get you a copy." Within a week, Anne Abernathy received a copy of the picture beautifully framed and ready for hanging.

"That was my first true impression of J. C.," Reverend Abernathy said, "a caring, sensitive person who picks up on a need and meets it."

In 1993 J. C. was ordained as a Southern Baptist minister in front of an overflowing congregation at Sunnylane Church. There were friends and family from Eufaula, friends from OU, friends from the Fellowship of Christian Athletes, and of course all of his friends who attended Sunnylane. Buddy Watts preached the ordination message. Few of the white folk at Sunnylane had ever heard a power-packed message from a black preacher, but they certainly heard one that day. Afterward, Helen Lucas walked up to the newly ordained minister and joked, "You may be a good speaker, J. C., but you'll never preach like your daddy!"

The world of politics eventually pulled J. C. away from Sunnylane and the close friendships he once had there. Nelda now serves on the board of Frankie Watts's ministry organization, More Grace, which arranges opportunities for J. C.'s wife to speak to women's groups around the country. Every once in a while, in spite of the busy hectic life of a congressman, J. C. will call Nelda to ask about her and her family. Before they hang up, Nelda has a habit of reminding J. C., "Remember Whose you are, J. C."

She knows he knows—but a reminder never hurts.

# 6

# OKLAHOMA POLITICS

❧

$I$N 1980, WHILE J. C. was still a journalism major at Oklahoma, he had been assigned to cover a political debate between two men who were running for the U.S. Senate. One was a young Republican business-man from Ponca City; the other was the Democratic mayor of Oklahoma City.

J. C. listened intently and with an open mind. He was shocked to walk away from the debate realizing he had agreed with the Republican candidate (Don Nickles, who won the election and went on to become a U.S. senator from Oklahoma). Most of the black people that J. C. knew, especially his family and friends from Eufaula, were Democrats.

"I thought being a Democrat was my birthright," J. C. explained to the *Washington Post* in 1997. "My father was a Democrat. All the blacks I knew were Democrats. My uncle had been president of the state NAACP. I had a legacy to uphold."

The legacy J. C. referred to was not just a local attitude. Only 8.7 percent of African Americans in the entire nation are registered members of the Republican Party. Out of more than 8,000 elected black officials in the United States, less than 1 per-cent are Republicans. The deep division stems back to the tumultuous civil rights era of the 1960s, when the Democrats became the party that favored civil rights. The Republican party leaned toward "states'

*After being elected Oklahoma Corporation Commissioner as a Republican, J. C. Watts was invited to meet with President George Bush, who visited Oklahoma during his 1992 reelection campaign. Watts later seconded Bush's nomination at the 1992 Republican National Convention in August.*

rights," allowing individual states to set their own laws and standards on race. Since that time, no Republican presidential candidate has ever received more than 15 percent of the black vote.

In Oklahoma the difference between the goals and values of Democrats and those of Republicans has never been as deep as it is in other states. While geographically the state straddles the South and Midwest, it is culturally more Southern. Most Oklahomans are considered conservative, Democrats included. Overall, Oklahoma Democrats are more likely to vote Republican than Democrats in any other state. However the one true division has always been according to race. The black community has historically looked to the Democratic party to be the answer for the working man and the poor. The Reverend Wade Watts, J. C.'s uncle, once referred to the Republican party as having a philosophy that violates the interests of "poor people, working people, common people."

The debate that J. C. had witnessed between the two candidates in 1980 continued to bother him. The conflict between his Democratic heritage and his conservative beliefs stayed with him for nine years. The words of Don Nickles "resonated with the values on which I had been raised," J. C. said. "[These were] all the things my dad always taught me: work hard, play fair, be responsible, pay your own way. . . . I couldn't believe a Republican—let alone a white Republican—would be agreeing with my father."

The inner conflict didn't come to a head until the fall of 1988, after J. C. cast his vote for the Democratic Party's presidential candidate, Michael Dukakis—a candidate he didn't like very much. "I told myself I would never again vote against my true convictions," he said. In 1989, J. C. switched to the Republican Party. The decision would prove to be a monumental one. It would also be a difficult one

to explain to family and friends—especially his staunchly Democratic father and uncle. "I was probably more afraid [to break the news to my father] than of facing any lineman in my college or professional football career," J. C. admitted to the *Washington Post* in 1997. "But he took it fairly well." Politics would become a subject the two men would avoid for many years to come.

"I don't see any reason for there to be a problem in the family over politics," Buddy commented, adding jokingly, "A black man voting for the Republicans makes about as much sense as a chicken voting for Colonel Sanders." Wade Watts, however, wasn't quite as gentle. He would later state that he felt the Republican Party "brainwashed," his nephew, and

*While still a college student, Watts heard Don Nickles (shown at right in a 1998 photo) debate a Democratic opponent during his race for a U.S. Senate seat. The words of the Oklahoma Republican inspired J. C. to learn more about the Republican Party.*

accused the party leaders of "showboating" J. C.

J. C. Watts had kept a high profile in Oklahoma, and by the late 1980s he had become a spokesman for many organizations, including the YMCA, Big Brothers/Big Sisters, the Fellowship of Christian Athletes, the Muscular Dystrophy Association, and various anti-drug programs. Everywhere he went, people liked and respected him. He was often encouraged to become involved in politics. The idea wasn't a new one; J. C. had thought about politics as a career since he was in college. But he was waiting for the right time and the right place. That came in 1990.

In Oklahoma, the powerful Corporation Commission regulates the state's energy industry, utility and telephone rates, and trucking industry. It is also responsible for protecting Oklahoma's environment. The commission sees to it that people are offered fair prices for oil and gas, and that no one energy company charges more than another. Because Oklahoma is one of the largest oil-producing states in the country, the Corporation Commission has a lot of power and influence in statewide politics. The commission is run by three elected officials.

In 1990 Commissioner James Townsend, a Democrat, was coming to the end of his six-year term. The Democratic and Republican parties would hold primary elections (these determine each party's candidate) in August, with a general election in November.

J. C. began seriously considering entering the race for commissioner. His background in the oil and gas industries attracted him to the position. (In spite of many problems and downturns, his company, Watts Energy in Norman, was still intact.) He analyzed his potential opponents as carefully as he had once studied the defenses of opposing teams. He didn't want to be involved in the race if there was no chance of success. "I think it has to be a winable deal," he commented. "You don't get into a statewide race to lose."

Even though he knew he would be the underdog, J. C. chose to enter the race for corporation commissioner as a Republican candidate. This move made him the first black candidate of either party to seek statewide office in Oklahoma.

The campaign was a rough one, because the incumbent Townsend decided to run for reelection. J. C. chose to run on the issues, promising to get rid of the "long entrenched good-ole boys." He accused the agency bureaucrats of delaying regulatory hearings, causing businesses to move jobs to states where the decision-making process was speedier. J. C. promised to shape things up while treating both consumers and producers fairly.

Having been in the oil and gas industry, J. C. knew that the position of corporation commissioner was a controversial one. He knew that he would have to make unpopular decisions. But, he contended, he'd been under the gun before as a football quarterback, saying there's no hotter seat in Oklahoma than that. "If people have been treated with integrity and with professionalism and feel they haven't been politicked or good-old-boyed, I think they can stomach those decisions much better," he explained.

Watts proved that underdogs can come out on top as he won a three-way race in the general election, garnering 50.3 percent of the vote. The victory was exciting. It proved that the people of Oklahoma believed and trusted J. C. Watts.

When J. C. was installed as corporation commissioner, Buddy and Wade Watts were both there. In his remarks to the crowd, J. C. noted that his father and uncle would never have dreamed their son and nephew would become a corporation commissioner. The he added, "especially as a Republican." The loud "Amen" that came from the two black preachers brought a ripple of laughter to the crowd.

Although he'd been retired from professional football for over five years, in 1991 football came back into J. C.'s life with a great flourish. In September he learned he was being inducted into the Orange Bowl Hall of Honor. Watts had been one of only two players in Orange Bowl history to be named Most Valuable Player twice. Many of his football accomplishments, which he had thought were long buried, once more came to light. He was honored at the Orange Bowl luncheon in Miami on December 30, and was a guest of honor at the Orange Bowl Parade and at the game on New Year's Day. This time he could relax with none of the tension of having to perform on the field.

After being elected commissioner, J. C. continued working as youth pastor at Sunnylane. The kids remembered that he was just as much fun as he'd always been. He also was attentive to his family, which had grown to seven with the birth of two more children, a daughter named Julie, born in 1990, and a son named Julius Caesar Watts III (nicknamed "Trey," for three), born in 1991.

However, while things were the same at home, they were changing elsewhere. J. C.'s election had attracted the attention of national Republican leaders. To his surprise, in June 1991 he was invited to Houston to attend a special meeting of these leaders. A news story indicated that J. C. would speak to the GOP group on "the government's role in fostering business development, creating opportunity, and protecting families."

The national interest was not a passing fancy. The next invitation he received was to second the nomination of President Bush at the Republican National Convention in August 1992.

"It's hard to put into words how excited and honored I am," J. C. said. "It's quite an honor for an old kid from Eufaula, Oklahoma."

Commissioner Watts had met the president previously when Bush made a campaign stop in Oklahoma City. They rode together in the limousine to Tinker

Air Force Base. J. C. remembered that he talked to the president about "youth programs, politics, and a little football."

By now, Commissioner Watts was an accomplished public speaker, and he didn't feel at all nervous to give his speech before thousands of people at the Republican Convention. He even wrote the speech himself. "My parents taught me to love America for her promise," he began. "The University of Oklahoma football team taught me to love America for her openness. But it was the party of Abraham Lincoln that taught me that America really is the land of opportunity. I am a Republican because ours is the only party founded on an idea—the idea of freedom, emancipation, opportunity." J. C. went on to compare the Republican and Democratic parties, and called Democratic candidate Bill Clinton "a failed governor of a small state."

Although three other convention delegates had

*Republicans cheer at the 1992 convention as George Bush receives his party's nod for the presidential campaign. J. C. Watts was on the stage at the time, after seconding the incumbent president's nomination.*

*J. C. waits in line to vote. In 1993, he was elected chairman of the three-member board of commissioners; the next year, he decided to run for the House of Representatives.*

seconded Bush's nomination, Watts's speech caused the most positive reactions. Oklahoma City delegate Kaye Kird stated that "J. C. is . . . a perfect example of what the Republican party is."

In January 1993, J. C. Watts Jr. was elected chairman of the three-man Oklahoma Corporation Commission. This showed that he was still trusted at home as well as on a national level.

His term as commissioner was not without problems, however. An FBI investigation revealed that one of the commissioners had been acting as an informant in a probe of the agency. A former commissioner had been indicted in a bribery case and was awaiting trial. However, J. C. was never implicated in the scandal, and it did not affect his popularity with the public.

Later that year, rumors began to circulate that J. C. was considering a higher public office, such as lieutenant governor of the state. This turned out to be more than a rumor, as Watts did indeed give the race a serious look. Even though he had received a good deal of support, J. C. decided against it by November 1993.

Next came rumors that he might run for the U. S. Senate. One of Oklahoma's two senate seats would become vacant in 1994 if the incumbent, David Boren, accepted a position as president of J. C.'s alma mater, the University of Oklahoma.

By the summer of 1994, J. C. had decided not to seek election to the Senate. Instead he decided to run for a seat in the House of Representatives. He would represent Oklahoma's Fourth District, where the incumbent congressman, Dave McCurdy, had decided to leave his post and run for the U. S. Senate. "I have received a great many calls and letters from both Republicans and Democrats in the Fourth District encouraging me to run," the commissioner told reporters. When he officially announced that he would seek the Fourth District seat in Congress, J. C. Watts became the first African American from Oklahoma to ever run as a Republican for a seat in the House of Representatives.

# 7

## TO WASHINGTON, D. C.

T HE FOURTH CONGRESSIONAL District of Oklahoma is located in the southwest quadrant of Oklahoma. It is made up of ten counties, as well as a small portion of Oklahoma County. The district has a wide economic diversity, as well as vast agricultural assets and products. Included in the district are several of the area's largest employers: Altus Air Force Base, Fort Sill Army Post, General Motors, Goodyear, Tinker Air Force Base, and the University of Oklahoma.

The district is considered one of the most liberal in the state; Watts is a conservative. The district is 93 percent white; Watts is black. The district is 69 percent Democratic; Watts is Republican. With those kinds of odds, most people would never even try to enter such a congressional race, let alone expect to win. But J. C. Watts Jr. had already learned to perform under pressure. He jumped into the campaign with enthusiasm.

Watts's opponent, David Perryman, an Oklahoma City attorney and OU graduate, went on the attack. He ran a television ad in which he posed with a pig to demonstrate his support of farmers. Then he held up a football and said of J. C. Watts, "This is the only pigskin he ever carried." Perryman also ran an ad showing a high school photo of J. C. sporting a large Afro haircut, which was popular in the '70s.

*David Perryman, Watts's opponent in the 1994 fourth District race, attacked J. C. with negative advertising, including one that showed him as a young quarterback with his large Afro haircut. However, the strategy backfired, because people felt Perryman was making race an issue.*

However this ad backfired, according to an Oklahoma City publisher named Richard Hefton. "People thought [Perryman] was making an issue of J. C.'s race and they didn't like that." Later, J. C. joked about the TV spot, saying, "You know, I worked pretty hard on my Afro and he made fun of it."

J. C. Watts ran on issues of family values, welfare reform, a balanced budget, and a strong military. He told the voters about "sustaining the magic of America." In a campaign speech, he said, "Friends, we live in the greatest land on the face of this earth. People fight to get to America, the land of opportunity. The key to sustaining the magic of America is family, community, morality, responsibility, strong education, and bringing God back into the mainstream of things." He made his strong religious convictions clear, stating that the Bible is "the only consistent social policy we've had for the past 2,000 years."

Oklahomans of the Fourth District liked J. C. Watts and they appreciated his message. On November 8, 1994, the voters elected Julius Caesar Watts Jr. to represent them in the House of Representatives. He was the first African-American Republican candidate from a Southern state to win a seat in Congress since the Reconstruction period that followed the Civil War.

Some critics did claim that J. C. Watts had won the election simply because he was a well-known athlete. As further proof that the name recognition a sports career provides can help further a person's political aspirations, these critics pointed out that another Oklahoman, Steve Largent, had also won a seat in the House of Representatives in 1994. Largent has just retired after a Hall of Fame pro football career with the Seattle Seahawks.

"My athletic experience was a very good teacher," Watts responded. "It taught me endurance, patience, delayed gratification. And being a quarterback teaches you to have tough skin. Regardless of what people are saying, if you stay focused, things will work out. Athletics teaches you that you can lose without being a loser."

J. C. and Frankie Watts did not want his new position to affect their family too much. They decided to maintain their Norman home to keep their five children's lives as normal as possible. Congressman Watts rented a modest apartment in D.C. and flew back home to Oklahoma on weekends.

Watts was one of many Republican candidates elected in 1994. Voters were disgusted by President Bill Clinton's policy failures—including a plan for national health care—and various scandals associated with the administration. In response they voted for GOP candidates in record numbers, sweeping the

Republicans into control of both houses of Congress for the first time in 40 years.

As a freshman congressman, J. C. spent his first year learning the ins and outs of the political system. He worked hard to maintain his conservative beliefs and viewpoint. He was selected by the Speaker of the House, Newt Gingrich, to be cochair of the Minority Issues and Outreach Task Force. And he sparked a mild controversy by deciding not to join a group of African-American congressmen called the Black Caucus. He said that he did not want to be singled out by his skin color. Watts was the first black congressman not to join the Caucus since it had been formed 24 years earlier.

J. C. Watts did write and sponsor one important piece of legislation as a freshman congressman: the America Community Renewal Act (ACRA). He was assisted by Congressman Jim Talent of Missouri. ACRA represented J. C.'s desire to aid and support poorer communities. In spite of a growing, thriving national economy, Congressman Watts felt deep concern that the inner cities were trapped in a downward spiral of poverty and crime.

In order to lay the foundation for the legislation, the two congressmen traveled hundreds of miles and visited the inner cities, talking to social workers. From these discussions with the people who could see the problems of the cities most clearly, the congressmen learned what was working, and what was not working. "It is their insights and experiences that permeate this legislation," Talent explained.

The America Community Renewal Act was designed to strengthen local schools, neighborhoods, and communities. The wheels of progress in government, however, grind very slowly. ACRA was not passed that first year, but Watts and Talent never gave up. Instead, they worked tirelessly to strengthen their research, and to make the public aware of the bill. An article cowritten by Talent and Watts presented harsh

statistics about the problems of the inner cities, and reminded readers that the worst problem was hopelessness. "Beyond the statistics, however, are broken men and women, searching for hope in communities dominated by despair." The America Community Renewal Act, they wrote, would provide hope to people in the blighted communities.

Watts was also passionate about other Congressional issues, including a balanced budget, improved education, and a strengthened national defense. And whenever it was applicable, he spoke out about his faith. "I think we've had a theological switch here in the last 30 years," he said in a 1995 interview. "I cannot support a political agenda that says there's nothing absolutely right and nothing absolutely wrong."

*J. C. Watts speaks about the Republican "Contract with America," a program of proposed legislation that the GOP freshmen in the 104th Congress had promised to vote on within the first 100 days.*

That the public appreciated his efforts in Congress was demonstrated in the numerous awards that he received: the 1996 Junior Chamber of Commerce's Ten Outstanding Young Americans Award, the Jefferson Award for promoting economic prosperity and free enterprise, the Christian Coalition's Friend of the Family Award, and the YMCA's Strong Kids, Strong Families, Strong Communities plaque.

Even the man who had been the representative from Oklahoma's fourth district before J. C. Watts had good things to say about the young congressman. Dave McCurdy, a Democrat who had resigned the post in 1994 to run unsuccessfully for the U.S. Senate, commented that J. C. is "a nice guy with star quality." He added that J. C. was respected "because he defies images. Things are somehow different when he says it, somehow softer."

J. C. Watts's first two-year term in Congress was drawing to a close in the summer of 1996. He decided to run for reelection in the fall. As he prepared his own campaign, he was asked to cochair the election committee of the GOP's presidential candidate, Bob Dole. At the Republican National Convention in August 1996, he was further thrust into the national spotlight when he introduced Dole to millions of national television viewers.

In the national election a few months later, voters chose to stay with President Bill Clinton. The incumbent received 49 percent of the vote to Dole's 41 percent. In Oklahoma's Fourth District, the voters also decided to stay with their current congressman, reelecting J. C. Watts with 58 percent of the vote.

In February 1997, a few weeks after Clinton's second inaugural, the president was scheduled to give a speech to the nation. This speech, known as the State of the Union Address, is an annual event in which the president talks about what's going on in the nation's government, and what citizens can expect from government in the next year. Afterward it is common for a member of the opposing political party to comment on the content of the president's State of the Union Address. Often, this response will try to refute the president's claims or make people think twice about his plans for the future.

In the winter of 1996, Bob Dole had been the leading Republican, so he gave the party's rebuttal to Clinton's State of the Union Address. In 1997, GOP leader New Gingrich asked J. C. Watts to give the party's response to the speech. This was another sign of J. C.'s growing importance in the party. He was the youngest congressman ever to give the response, and the first African American.

"J. C. was an obvious choice," commented Gingrich. "He's a natural leader with special gifts who can communicate the values most Americans are committed to, namely family, faith, and community. He also offers a strong voice on a broad range of issues from balancing the budget, to winning the war against drugs, to ensuring our national security."

On February 4, 1997, J. C. Watts appeared on national television following Clinton's State of the Union Address. Watts opened by saying, "I'm going to try to use my words tonight and my time not to confuse issues but to clarify them; not to obscure my philosophy and my party's, but to illuminate it, because the way I see it the purpose of politics is to lead, not to mislead.

"The strength of America is not in Washington, the strength of America is at home in lives well lived in the land of faith and family. The strength of America is not on Wall Street but on Main Street. . . . It's not in Congress, it's in the city hall."

The congressman then went on to outline the objectives of the Republican party. First was to help the country by returning to spiritual, traditional, and family values. Another objective was to pass legislation amending the U.S. Constitution so that the federal government would be required to

*Responding to President Clinton's 1997 State of the Union Address, J. C. Watts discusses the objectives and beliefs of his party. "I didn't get my values from Washington," he said. "I got my values growing up in a black neighborhood on the east side of the tracks where money was scarce but dreams were plentiful and love was all around."*

balance the budget. Later in the speech, he pointed out the individual responsibility of each person. "We must all accept our share of responsibility. . . . We must be a people who dare to take responsibility for our hatred and fears and ask God to heal us from within; and we must be a people of prayer, a people who pray as if the strength of our nation depended on it, because it does."

Watts closed his speech by quoting a line from President John Kennedy's inaugural address: "'Let us go forth to lead the land we love, knowing that here on Earth, God's work truly must be our own.' I say amen to that."

Reactions to the speech were quick in coming, and most were positive and accepting of what the congressman had to say. "Congressman Watts spoke to things that matter in the lives of every American family: values, work, living within your means, and character. He spoke in language that we use around the kitchen table," said Pete du Pont, former Republican Governor of Delaware. And *Headway* magazine said that the speech received "positive reviews from both political friends and opponents, something about which few GOP elected officials can boast."

However, J. C.'s message was overshadowed somewhat by a controversy that had erupted the day of the speech. After Gingrich announced his choice of Watts to give the Republican response to the State of the Union Address, the media focused on the young congressman. A reporter from the *Washington Post* wrote a long story about J. C. that appeared on February 4, 1997, the day of the speech. A comment in Ken Ringle's article, headlined "Carrying the GOP Ball," caused a flurry of controversy. J. C. had told the reporter that he had nothing but contempt for certain African-American leaders who profit from poverty and racial conflict. He called them "race-hustling poverty pimps." In the *Post* story, the Reverend Jesse Jackson, a well-known civil rights leader, and Washington, D.C., mayor Marion Barry, were cited as examples.

Watts insisted he had not specifically named anyone when he was interviewed, inferring that the names had been inserted by the reporter. The names were, after all, outside the quotation marks in the article. However, Jackson was incensed by the comment attributed to J. C. Watts. The article also led to a heated exchange between J. C. and Jackson's son, Jesse Jr., a Democratic member of Congress who represented Illinois.

Speaking in Watts's defense, Congressman Mark Foley, a Republican from Florida said, "It's very unlike him, very unlike J. C. Because I know he's a very compassionate and straightforward individual."

J. C. did eventually issue an apology to Jackson. However many people felt he should not have done so. Robert Woodson, president of the National Center for Neighborhood Enterprise, was one of them. "I think he needs to challenge and not apologize for doing it," Woodson said in an interview. Willie A. Richardson, publisher of *Headway* magazine, echoed those sentiments. "I was disappointed that he chose to apologize to Rev. Jesse Jackson for something that Watts did not even do. . . . Nevertheless, I understood Watts' motivation. If he hadn't, the story would have been kept alive."

While some inferred that a rift between Watts and Jackson meant that J. C. was opposed by the

NAACP as well, that was not entirely true. In fact, NAACP president Kweisi Mfume was counted as a close friend and supporter of J. C. Watts. Mfume called Watts a statesman and noted that he had genuine respect for the Oklahoma congressman. "The fact that J. C. and I are in different parties really doesn't matter," Mfume noted. He said that he and Watts had shared many conversations, not about their differences, but "about the future of America."

The month following the State of the Union response found Watts being honored at a gathering at a hotel in Washington, D.C. More than 200 friends, family members, and supporters attended the "Salute to J. C. Watts" on March 15, 1997. The editors of the conservative magazine *Headway* chose to honor Watts because, in the words of Willie Richardson, "We share the same philosophy. His emphasis on the importance of family coincides with our placing 'strong families' as item number one on our political philosophy."

Among the special guests were J. C.'s high school coach Paul Bell and Sunnylane Baptist pastor Jerry Don Abernathy, both of whom shared stories about the congressman that brought laughter and tears to those in attendance. Also present at the tribute were J. C.'s wife, Frankie, and three of their five children.

The significance of the tribute, according to J. C., spoke volumes about the appeal and acceptance of his political philosophy. "It makes a bold statement about blacks who happen to be Republicans," he said. "It means it's OK if we don't agree with the status quo. We don't have to buy into any group identity. . . . Yes I'm a Republican, but I'm also just as concerned about the poor. I just see a different way of solving the problem."

Throughout J. C.'s second term in Congress he continued to work hard for passage of the America Community Renewal Act, in spite of the fact that it had never made it out of committee. He was able,

however, to see success in the area of national defense in the summer of 1997. The house passed a $268 billion defense bill by a wide margin, 304 to 120. The victory was especially sweet to J. C. because the bill included language that would require the Air Force to transfer thousands of aircraft repair jobs to Tinker Air Force Base, which was in the district he served, and two other depots. In addition, Oklahoma bases would get several million dollars in construction money. J. C. said the bill was good for the Fourth District, and it was also "good for the overall defense of the nation."

In November 1997, the *Tulsa World* carried a banner headline that read "Sooner to Make Presidential Run?" The article referred to an invitation

*Representative Jim Talent of Missouri cosponsored the America Community Renewal Act with J. C. Watts. The Oklahoma Republican felt that ACRA was his most important legislation.*

that J. C. had received from the Iowa Republican Party to be a speaker at one of the group's premier events. Historically Iowa has been an important spot for presidential hopefuls to test their strength, and past speakers at this event had included George Bush, Bob Dole, and Jack Kemp. Steve Grubbs, the chairman of the Iowa Republican Party, said that he'd begged Watts's office for six months to have him scheduled at the event. "We really only invite the people we consider the top national Republicans," Grubbs said.

Grubbs commented that J. C. Watts should consider a national campaign for president in the year 2000. "I've seen a lot of potential presidential candidates come through our state, and if Congressman Watts decides to throw his hat in the ring, he will immediately be ranked near the top," he said. J. C. did not indicate that he was thinking about a presidential run, but did not rule it out either, saying, "If your country calls, it would be like a call from your mother."

For J. C. to hear his name in connection to the presidency started becoming commonplace. At a public policy seminar held in Washington, D.C., and attended by 400 Christian ministers, well-known evangelist Jerry Falwell prefaced Watts's remarks by saying, "Ladies and gentlemen, let me introduce you to the man who just may be the first African-American president of the United States." The response was a thunderous standing ovation, but once again Watts was low-key about his intentions. "I've never needed to have anything other than the title of 'Dad' in front of my name to tell me who I am and what I should stand for."

Family continued to be highly important to J. C. During his first term in office, he spent nearly every weekend at home in Norman with Frankie and their children. In a 1996 interview, he quipped that he'd seen the movie *Beauty and the Beast* 119 times, because his youngest daughter loved the story.

In September 1997, in St. Louis, Missouri, Frankie Watts received the "Full-Time Homemaker of the Year Award" presented by the Eagle Forum. Upon receiving the award, she thanked her mother, who had also been a full-time homemaker, and whom Frankie referred to as her role model. Then she thanked her husband, J. C. Watts, for making it possible for her to be a stay-at-home mom.

Stop Dis[crimi]nation Against [Na]tive Ameri[cans]

SUPPORT
INDIAN
GAMING
SAVE THE DREAM

Save the Dream MARCH
Selma 1965 - Sacramento
OCTOBER 27, 1997

# 8

# AFFIRMATIVE ACTION

❦

IN 1961 PRESIDENT John Kennedy, recognizing the problem of discrimination against minorities in America, issued Executive Order 10925. This order established the President's Committee on Equal Employment Opportunity. It was intended to end discrimination in employment by the government and its contractors. For the first time, an initiative to help minorities was to be more than just words. It was to take "affirmative action," or appropriate steps to eradicate widespread practices of racial, religious, and ethnic discrimination. The Civil Rights Act of 1964 broadened this principle to include any program or activity receiving federal financial assistance.

In the 1970s an official commission was set up to enforce racial quotas. This meant that federally funded businesses and organizations were required by law to hire a certain number of minorities (both racial minorities, such as African Americans, and women). Although these measures were put in place to eliminate discrimination, they caused some people to complain about "reverse discrimination." Opponents believed that qualified applicants for jobs would be passed over because they were white males, while less-qualified persons might be hired simply to fill a federally ordered race- or gender-based quota. Thus began decades of controversy over affirmative action.

From the day he arrived in Washington, D.C.,

*The Reverend Jesse Jackson leads a group of marchers through the streets of Sacramento, California, in 1997, protesting against that state's stand on affirmative action.*

*The issue of affirmative action has been a divisive one; while J. C. Watts says affirmative action is a flawed system, he also does not want to see it eliminated until it can be replaced with a better alternative.*

Congressman Watts let it be known that he did not totally agree with affirmative action. His main reason for this attitude was that he did not believe society's problems could be solved by politicians. However, when many of his Republican colleagues were calling for legislation to abolish affirmative action, J. C. Watts stood virtually alone in a fight to save it.

A May 1998 *Washington Post* article stated, "Even

as Republican leaders have repeatedly given their blessing to measures aimed at rolling back [affirmative action], the lone black Republican in the House has served as a bulwark against any dramatic change."

As far back as the summer of 1995, Watts was actively opposing the repeal of affirmative action legislation. The Equal Opportunity Act of 1995, introduced in the Senate by Bob Dole and in the House by Florida Republican Charles Canady, would have eliminated affirmative action and put nothing in its place to prevent race- or gender-based discrimination. Watts refused to support the legislation. Later Dole let the Equal Opportunity Act drop, and no one else in the House pushed it. Watts's willingness to express his doubts about affirmative action and the Republican's attack on it showed political courage. An article in *Washington Monthly* pointed out that it was rare to hear a politician admit that he doesn't have all the answers.

In November 1997 Congressman Canady sponsored another bill that would reverse the affirmative action practices of the past. This legislation was designed to prohibit the federal government from considering race or gender as a factor in federal hiring and contracting. When the bill came up for debate in the House, Watts and Republican Henry Bonilla of Texas objected strongly to the measure.

"It was his objection . . . that really convinced us to hold up on this and talk about it more," said Georgia congressman John Linder. Eventually, the Canady bill died in committee.

J. C. Watts is no fan of the affirmative action policy. In public forums, he has often criticized affirmative action, and once became involved in a verbal sparring match on this issue with the Reverend Jesse Jackson and former NAACP chairman Julian Bond on the NBC program *Meet the Press*. However he has always reminded his Republican colleagues that they cannot afford to abolish affirmative action without first putting into place an alternative plan to help minorities.

Watts demonstrated this opinion in May 1998, when a bill that would deny federal funds to public colleges and universities that rely on affirmative action in their admissions policies came up for a vote in the House of Representatives. The legislation had been proposed by a Republican congressman from California named Frank Riggs. In the weeks before the House vote on the measure, Watts joined forces with another African-American congressman, Democrat John Lewis of Georgia. Together, Watts and Lewis wrote a letter that they sent to all the members of the House, urging them to vote against the Riggs bill. "This is not the time to eliminate the one tool we have—imperfect though it may be—to help level the playing field for many minority youth," they wrote.

Their efforts were successful, as the bill was defeated in the House by a vote of 171 to 249.

It has been a source of frustration for J. C. Watts that while the Republicans in Congress were trying to abolish affirmative action, his plan to help minorities and revitalize cities, the America Community Renewal Act, remained dormant. The first version of the bill never made it out of committee. "I would sure like to see them throw their support behind community renewal, and put the same kind of effort behind that effort that they put behind Riggs," Watts has remarked.

Affirmative action often puts J. C. Watts in a difficult position. The leadership of his party believes that most Americans want the affirmative action policies abolished. Democrats, on the other hand, have never fully understood how an African American can oppose a policy that attempts to compensate for years of discrimination against blacks, or that Watts's views on affirmative action differ from most members of the GOP.

In a *Washington Post* article published shortly after the Riggs balloting, a Democratic congressman from South Carolina named James Clyburn admitted that he and others had changed their minds about J. C. when they read an interview with him in the *Financial Times*. According to the article, Clyburn told Congressman Bennie Thompson of Mississippi, "We have not done right by J. C. Watts. When you read what he has to say, he was exactly where we were on the end result." And even though Tom Coburn, like J. C. a Republican congressman from Oklahoma, voted for the Riggs amendment, he was glad that Watts had raised the issue. "That's why J. C. is good to have around. It's all about reconciliation in this country. We're never going to solve these problems up here [in Washington], because they're problems of the heart."

"I work very hard not to have to play the role of the black Republican, the black conservative," says J. C. Watts. "Like it or not, people force me to play the role of the black Republican."

While the disagreements about affirmative action are certainly not over, Republicans acknowledge that it is not time to overturn affirmation action. This is due in part to Congressman Watts's firm stand, and his influence with both the House leadership and with the rank-and-file members of Congress, according to the *Washington Post*. But it has been lonely fight. During the vote on the Riggs bill, the Republican congressmen clustered around a computer display to watch the votes being tabulated, while the Democrats huddled on their side of the aisle. J. C. Watts sat by himself.

# 9

# THIRD-TERM CONGRESSMAN

❧

THE SUMMER OF 1998 was one of the hottest
in Oklahoma in over a decade. Several straight days
of 100-degree temperatures and no rain created an
extensive drought in the farmlands. During this heat
wave, J. C. Watts found himself in a hot political race
as well. His third campaign for Congress was hotly
contested by a Democrat from Norman named Ben
Odom. Odom said he decided to run because Watts
was doing "a great job of being a celebrity and a rot-
ten job of being a congressman."

Odom decided to attack his popular opponent by
portraying him in a negative light. He ran television
ads claiming that when Watts was running for the
Oklahoma Corporation Commission, he had
accepted a bribe from a lobbyist named William
"Tater" Anderson. Odom also set up a site on the
Internet with negative information about J. C. Watts.

J. C. Watts reacted quickly to the allegations.
Although the investigation into the Corporation
Commission had resulted in three indictments in
1991, Watts had never been connected to the scandal. His campaign manager, Chad Alexander, issued
a press release stating that the FBI, federal prosecu-
tors, and a federal grand jury had reviewed Watts's
friendship with Anderson and found no evidence of
wrongdoing. A 1994 letter from assistant U.S. Attorney John E. Green further revealed that there had

never been any indication that J. C. Watts was involved in the scandal. The congressman himself responded to the accusations by saying, "Why is it my opponent would go and take eight-year-old information and put it on an oxygen tank and get it to breathe again when I've been cleared of this stuff?"

When Rev. Jerry Don Abernathy of Sunnylane Baptist heard the negative ads that Odom was airing, he filmed a TV spot in support of J. C. in which he said: "J. C. Watts never met a person he wouldn't help, nor had a bill that he didn't pay, nor made a mistake that he didn't admit and try to correct."

Odom also accused J. C. of consistently voting with unpopular House Speaker Newt Gingrich more than 90 percent of the time. "Newt Gingrich votes with the 4th District of Oklahoma over 90 percent of the time," J. C. responded. "I don't care who votes to cut people's taxes, balance the budget, support education and strengthen the military, I'm going to support it."

By the time the hot Oklahoma summer faded into a somewhat cooler autumn, J. C. had earned support from Democrats and Republicans alike throughout the Fourth District. On the night of November 3, at a victory rally at the Holiday Inn in Norman, Oklahoma, a beaming J. C. Watts was rejoicing in his election to a third term in Congress. In each subsequent election, the voters had given him a higher margin of victory. This time, he received a hefty 61 percent of the vote. Early on in his career, J. C. had said he would run for Congress only three terms. But now this appeared to be a promise he might not keep. He said he would leave the decision to remain in Congress or to leave in 2000 up to the voters.

But J. C.'s success in Oklahoma was the exception, rather than the rule, for GOP congressional candidates in the 1998 election. A backlash over what some voters perceived as Republican harassment of

President Bill Clinton over the Monica Lewinsky affair and other controversies allowed the Democrats to pick up a number of seats in the House of Representatives.

House Speaker Newt Gingrich took the blame for the dismal showing of Republicans across the country. In a surprise move, he resigned from office on the Friday after the election. In a statement, the 20-year veteran of Congress said, "I urge my colleagues to pick leaders who can both reconcile and discipline, who can work together and communicate effectively." Gingrich's resignation sent shock waves through the GOP members of the House of Representatives, and they began seeking new leaders for the party's important positions.

J. C. Watts decided to run for chairman of the House Republican Conference, the fourth highest position in the party's leadership. The conference chairman presides over the organizational forum at the outset of each new Congress, at which resolutions, rules, and procedures are established. He or she also calls meetings of the conference and provides a forum for discussions, debate, and informational briefings on issues of concern to the members; coordinates the public relations efforts of party allies to get out the party's message; and publishes the *Legislative Digest* and related documents on legislative issues. The position had been held by Congressman John Boehner, a Republican from Ohio.

J. C. chose to make the announcement of his run for the position from his Norman, Oklahoma, office

*J. C. waits to hear the results of his 1998 race for reelection at a party in Oklahoma City. The Republican easily won reelection for a third term, garnering 61 percent of the vote.*

because "this is the model I want to duplicate," he said in a released statement. "In Oklahoma, we shoot straight and tell it like it is. I have learned all my values and beliefs right here." Another congressman, George Radanovich of California, also announced that he would challenge Watts for the position, but a few days later Radanovich changed his mind and pulled out of the race. When he did, he threw his support behind Congressman Watts.

When the House voted on leadership positions on November 18, 1998, J. C. Watts became conference chairman. As chairman, Watts would help shape the party's message, focus on member services, and run the weekly closed-door meetings in which lawmakers debate their most pressing legislative issues.

In a syndicated column, Arianna Huffington mentioned the slurs and attacks that had been made against J. C. as he put in his bid for the position. She quoted Watts's reply to media questions about these accusations: "I regret that the demands of my transition into the office of chairman of the House Republican Conference do not allow me time to go over this ground again."

"Hallelujah!" Huffington wrote, "Let these words be forever enshrined as the appropriate response to forever rehashing the flawed pasts of flawed human beings who seek public office."

At the same time Watts was voted in as conference chairman, Bob Livingston of Louisiana was selected as House Speaker and Dick Armey of Texas was chosen as House Majority Leader. Livingston, a 21-year veteran of the House, was a conservative who said that he would do his best to work with the Democrats.

As the House was setting its leadership positions in order, impeachment proceedings against President Clinton were shifting into high gear. (Impeachment is an accusation against a public official of misconduct in office.) After a hearing and a lengthy debate on evidence presented by Independent Counsel

Kenneth Starr, on December 19 a majority of House members voted to impeach the president. It was the first time in 130 years that a U.S. president had been impeached. The House ruled that Clinton had committed perjury (lied under oath) and had abused his power in efforts to cover up his relationship with a White House intern, Monica Lewinsky. After the House's impeachment decision, the U.S. Senate would hear the evidence and vote on the president's innocence or guilt. A two-thirds majority was

---

**THE DUTIES OF GOP
CONFERENCE CHAIRMAN**

In November 1998, J. C. Watts was selected as the chairman of the House Republican Conference. This is the fourth-highest position in the party's Congressional leadership. The duties of the GOP Conference Chairman are as follows:

- The chairman presides over the organizational forum at the outset of each new Congress, at which resolutions, rules, and procedures are agreed on.

- The chairman calls meetings of the conference and provides a forum for discussions, debate, and informational briefings on issues of concern to the members.

- The chairman coordinates outside allies and coalitions effort and assigns specific responsibilities to the vice chair and secretary.

- The chairman publishes the Legislative Digest and related documents on legislative issues.

- The chairman provides Republican members and staff with pending legislative, press and constituent service handbooks; provides analyses on pending bills and issues of significance.

- The chairman manages the resources of the conference in a manner that achieves the goals of the Republican members and carries out the policy objectives of the conference.

*After a series of tornadoes devastated Oklahoma in the summer of 1999, killing 43 people, J. C. Watts returned to his home state to do whatever he could to help.*

needed to convict the president on either charge.

As this was going on, the United States and Great Britain were making air strikes against the nation of Iraq. Accusations were made against the president that the bombing attacks were made solely to take attention off the impeachment proceedings.

The day after the House's impeachment proceedings began, a bomb of another sort was dropped on the House of Representatives. This time it was House Speaker Livingston—barely in the top leadership position for a month—who decided to resign. Once again the House of Representatives was in turmoil.

The reason Livingston quit was due in part to a threat made by Larry Flynt, the publisher of a pornographic magazine called *Hustler*. In a full-page ad in the *Wall Street Journal*, Flynt had offered a million dollars for information about "immoral" acts committed by anyone in Congress. This, he contended, was to show that some of the president's harshest critics had also behaved badly, but had not gotten caught.

Livingston in years past had "strayed from his marriage," as he put it. In spite of the fact that he'd received marital and spiritual counseling and that Bonnie Livingston, his wife of 33 years, and their family had forgiven him, he feared the damage the powerful Flynt might do. In the end, it was Bonnie who encouraged him to disclose his past and step down from the leadership position. She wanted him to be spared any further embarrassment. "What he did today was as much for [his wife] as for him and his country," commented the congressman from Louisiana, W. J. Tauzin. "His wife was in agony."

Announcing that he was stepping down from the post and leaving Congress, an emotional Livingston, speaking from the House floor said, "To my colleagues, my friends and most especially my wife and family, I have hurt you all deeply and I beg your forgiveness."

A few members of the House had sensed Livingston's resignation coming, but most were taken totally off guard. Now even as they were in the midst of the highly stressful impeachment proceedings, the House was like a family in mourning. David Obey, a Democrat from Wisconsin, was in tears as he said, "How many more good people are going to be destroyed? . . . What are we going to do? Line them all up and mow them down?" And Vic Fazio, a Democrat from California, said, "No one should be driven from office by the kind of position Mr. Livingston was put in. I think it's a terrible result."

Stepping in to take Livingston's place as House Speaker was J. Dennis Hastert, a Republican from rural Illinois. Before becoming a U.S. congressman in 1986, Hastert was a school teacher and coach in Yorkville, Illinois. While he was known as a quiet, behind-the-scenes type of congressman, Hastert was just the right person for the tumultuous times, according to his colleagues. He was described as being a firm but fair leader without a hint of scandal. "He is the best of what we think of as the old school," said Congressman Rick Lazio of New York.

In an interview he gave after being elected House Speaker, Hastert said, "I see myself as a person who throughout my career has listened to people and tried to understand the issues they want to talk about." He added, "I try to bring people together; I see that as my role." In his position of conference chairman, J. C. Watts would find himself working closely with this congressman from Illinois.

In the midst of the chaos and unrest, J. C. received word on December 16 that his Uncle Wade had passed away. The NAACP pioneer was remembered and honored in newspapers across the country. Wade Watts had joined the NAACP in 1935 when he was 17 years old. Eventually, he would serve as president of the Oklahoma chapter of the NAACP for 16 years. During President Lyndon B. Johnson's administration, Watts was appointed to the Civil Rights Commission.

During the 1950s and '60s, a time of unrest in the South over civil rights, Watts marched through Alabama with Martin Luther King Jr. The Ku Klux Klan often threatened Watts, and once burned down his church in McAlester, Oklahoma. His children went to school accompanied by armed guards. But he never let up his fight for equal rights for blacks.

"A lot of Daddy's causes weren't fought in McAlester, they were fought all over Oklahoma," said his daughter, Coluah Stanfield, after her father's death on December 14, 1998. "Daddy . . . fought for civil rights and Mama was left to raise us. We felt a loss in that. Then we saw a picture of him with Martin Luther King and we knew he was bigger than we could ever have dreamed of."

Oklahoma state senator Don Ross, an African American, called Wade Watts his "mentor and leader." He went on to say that Watts "traveled to trouble spots. He reinvigorated the [civil rights] movement." And Jack Henderson, past president of the Tulsa branch of the NAACP, commented that "the civil rights movement will have a void. There isn't anyone on the horizon who can fill those shoes."

J. C. spent the holidays with his family, and shared their grief at the death of his Uncle Wade. But when Congress reconvened after the New Year, he was focused on the biggest event in Washington, D.C.—the Senate impeachment trial of President Clinton. On February 12, 1999, the Senate voted the president not guilty of perjury by a 55–45 count. The senators were divided evenly on the obstruction of justice charge: 50 voted guilty and 50 not guilty. In both cases, the votes fell far short of the 67 needed for conviction. At last the impeachment proceedings

*In the spring of 1999, Texas governor George W. Bush asked J. C. to join his exploratory committee, a group of advisers who would help him decide whether to run for President in the next year's election. Other members of the committee, pictured here with Bush and his wife Laura, were Michigan governor John Engler (left) and Dr. Condi Rice (right).*

were over. Now J. C. and his colleagues could get back to the business of running the country.

J. C.'s mind was on the America Communities Renewal Act, which he'd been working on for a number of years. "I will come into the 106th Congress with this bill on the top of my personal agency," he said. "This is still my priority. Congress can no longer ignore the cries for help that are coming from America's inner cities and poor rural communities. The hour is late," he added. "The time to act is now."

Clarence Page, syndicated columnist for the *Chicago Tribune*, also mentioned ACRA in his column. He encouraged Republicans to take J. C. seriously for his ideas and not just for his complexion.

The bill was incorporated into the 1998 Taxpayer Relief Act, and was reintroduced in the House as H.R. 815, and in the Senate as S.B. 413. ACRA boasted 143 cosponsors and support from the mayors of some of America's largest cities: Rudolph Giuliani of New York, Richard Daley of Chicago, and Richard Riordan of Los Angeles. By March 1999 it was being processed through committee and would then go to the floor. The bill was passed simultaneously through both the House and the Senate but was vetoed by President Clinton, and Republicans in Congress did not have enough support to override the president's veto.

J. C. Watts seems almost old fashioned in this day and age. He admits that it all boils down to doing what your grandmother taught you. There are tried-and-true, simple philosophies that speak to a cross-section of Americans, going beyond boundaries of race, gender, socioeconomic standing, and political persuasion.

J. C. Watts believes in simple values: honesty, loyalty, commitment, and hard work. He is passionate about the issues that affect every American. At this point in his life, his position in Congress allows him a unique platform from which to speak. However, J. C. Watts was speaking and trying to make a difference before he was elected to Congress, and he will surely continue to do just that if he ever leaves office. "I don't need this job," J. C. has said about politics. He's often said he'd be happy as a farmer in Eufaula.

Speaking to the congregation at Crossroads Cathedral in Oklahoma City two days before the 1996 November election, he said, "I want to win the election on Tuesday, but if I don't, don't worry about me. God is going to grow me wherever He plants me."

No one who heard him doubted that Julius Caesar Watts Jr. was also *willing* to grow wherever God planted him.

After all, that's what J. C. Watts has been doing his entire life.

# CHRONOLOGY

1957   Born Julius Caesar Watts Jr. in Eufaula, Oklahoma

1973   Named first black quarterback of the Eufaula Ironheads

1976   Graduates from Eufaula High School; enters University of Oklahoma

1979   Becomes starting quarterback for the University of Oklahoma Sooners; guides team to a regular-season record of 10–1 and a berth in the Orange Bowl on New Year's Day

1980   Named Most Valuable Player at Orange Bowl after leading team to a 24–7 victory over Florida State University; gets off to shaky start in regular fall season but rebounds to lead Sooners to a 10–2 regular-season mark and another Orange Bowl berth

1981   Named Most Valuable Player in the Orange Bowl for the second time after directing last-minute 18–17 victory over FSU; graduates from the University of Oklahoma with a degree in journalism; snubs NFL's New York Jets and signs contract to play quarterback with the Ottawa Rough Riders of the Canadian Football League; joins the Rough Riders late in the season and leads squad into the championship game; after a near-upset of the heavily favored Edmonton team, selected Most Valuable Player of the Grey Cup

1986   Joins Toronto Argonauts of the CFL

1987   Becomes youth pastor at Sunnylane Baptist Church, Del City, Oklahoma

1990   Becomes the first African American elected to Corporation Commission in Oklahoma

1992   Inducted into the Orange Bowl Hall of Honor in January; speaks at the Republican National Convention in August

1993   Ordained as a Baptist minister at Sunnylane Baptist Church

1994   Elected to the House of Representatives from Oklahoma's Fourth Congressional District, the first African-American Republican congressman from the state

1996   Cochairs Bob Dole's national campaign for president; speaks at the Republican National Convention in San Diego, California; named one of the Top Ten Outstanding Young Americans for 1996 by the Junior Chamber of Commerce; reelected to Congress with 58 percent margin of votes

1997     Becomes the first African American to give his party's response to the annual State of the Union Address

1998     Reelected to Congress with 61 percent margin of votes

1999     Chosen as chairman of the Republican Conference, the first African American to hold the post

# Switching Party Loyalty

❧

When the headline "Honey, I Shrunk the Party" appeared in the July 3, 1995, issue of *Time* magazine, it was referring to a once-rare phenomenon that was becoming increasingly common—people switching their party affiliation. Many of the high-profile switches that occurred at this time were cases of Democrats who switched to the Republican party—much as J. C. Watts had done six years earlier. The difference was, these people were mostly elected officials—from local and state administrators to federal legislators. Many of them were Southern conservatives who felt alienated from the Democratic Party. "Clinton has all but abandoned [the Democrats] on the central issues of the day, especially the budget," *Time* reported, "making them a party without a President."

During the summer of 1995, four congressional Democrats resigned from the campaign committee. One of them, a representative from Texas named Greg Laughlin, said that the party "remains intolerant to variances [by individual members] from its national party message on any issue."

Following the November 1995 election, a press conference was held with one-time Democrats who were now Republican members of the House of Representatives. There were 11 members of this group, one of whom was J. C. Watts (standing at right in this photo from the press conference). On December 1, that number increased to 12 when Representative James A. Hayes of Louisiana announced his switch to the Republican Party. At the time, Hayes said that the Democratic Party "has no tolerance for everything I love about the independence and individuality of all Louisianans—Democrats, Republicans, and independents."

The party-switching trend has continued since then. In September 1998, the Republican National Committee announced that 367 officeholders had switched party allegiances since President Clinton took office in 1992. By September 1999, that number had swelled to 436.

Though the growing numbers may indicate otherwise, for

most the decisions did not come easily. Many of those who switched over had been lifetime Democrats. Larry Dolezal, a county commissioner in Montana, spoke for many when he discussed his decision to change parties: "It was a very difficult, soul-searching decision for me."

"The country is changing political attitudes," admitted Colorado Governor Roy Romer, the former chairman of the Democratic National Committee. "Across the South, a number of people have switched for survival or a comfort level. But the continued move of the Republican Party from right to far-right is going to cause a considerable loss of moderate Republicans, once moderate Republicans realize where their party now is."

# Three Lies—excerpts from a speech given by J. C. Watts' to young people

**Lie Number One:** "I'm entitled to one mistake"

We all *make* mistakes, but we are not *entitled* to mistakes. If you live your life believing that you are entitled to mistakes, you will bounce from wall to wall, never having any substance, never having any direction in your life.

**Lie Number Two:** "It will never happen to me"

My favorite basketball player, Magic Johnson, when he was tested positive for HIV said, "I guess I was naive—I never thought it would happen to me." Is it worth losing your reputation, losing your career, the rest of your life over what you've done wrong? It can happen to you!

**Lie Number Three:** "I've got plenty of time"

You don't have time. Today is the day you start preparing for the rest of your life. Good things happen to people who will work hard, pay the price, understand sacrifice and commitment, and will take pride in getting an education.

# J. C. Watts's college football statistics

| | RUSHING | | | | PASSING | | | | | |
|---|---|---|---|---|---|---|---|---|---|---|
| | Carries | Yards | Avg. | TD | Att. | Comp. | Percent | Yards | TD | Int. |
| 1976 | 6 | 20 | 3.3 | 0 | 0 | 0 | — | 0 | 0 | 0 |
| 1977 | Red Shirt | | | | | Red Shirt | | | | |
| 1978 | 42 | 204 | 4.9 | 6 | 38 | 13 | 34% | 227 | 2 | 4 |
| 1979 | 123 | 455 | 3.7 | 10 | 81 | 39 | 48% | 785 | 4 | 5 |
| 1980 | 163 | 663 | 4.1 | 18 | 78 | 35 | 45% | 905 | 2 | 10 |
| Totals | 334 | 1342 | 4.0 | 34 | 197 | 87 | 44% | 1917 | 8 | 19 |

# BIBLIOGRAPHY

Bonner, Mike. *How a Bill Is Passed*. Philadelphia: Chelsea House, 2000.

———. *How to Become an Elected Official*. Philadelphia: Chelsea House, 2000.

Collins, Rob. "Watts Ideology Based on Faith, Upbringing." *Norman Transcript*, 1 November 1998.

———. "Watts Battling for GOP Conference Chair." *Norman Transcript*, 9 November 1998.

Dickerson, John F. "The Watts Solution: Republicans Want To Show That They Care. J. C. Watts Is Their Man of the Moment." *Time* 152, no. 22 (30 November 1998).

Dubouoy, Sina, *Civil Rights Leaders*. New York: Facts on File, 1997.

Eilperin, Juliet. "Watts Walks a Tightrope on Affirmative Action." *Washington Post*, 12 May 1998.

Fulwood, Sam. "Republicans Cast Watts as Leader, Healer." *Los Angeles Times*, 22 February 1999.

Harlan, Kevin. "A Servant on the Hill." *Sharing the Victory*, January 1996.

Henry, Christopher E. *Presidential Conventions*. New York: Franklin Watts, 1996.

Hiller, Susan. "Football Players Turned Congressmen." *CFA Sidelines Magazine*, November 1995.

"J.C. Watts Is 1st Black Picked to Respond to a President's State of the Union Address," *Jet* 91 (February 24, 1997).

Kurkjian, Tim. "J.C. Watts," *Sports Illustrated* 81 (21 November 1994): 55.

Lawton, Kim A. "America's First Black President?" *Connection Magazine*, February 1998.

Lovitt, Chip. *Dallas Cowboys*. Mankato, Minn.: Creative Education, 1997.

Lucas, Eileen, *Cracking The Wall: the Struggles of the Little Rock Nine*. Minneapolis: Carolrhoda Books, 1997.

Morin, Isobel. *Impeaching the President*. Brookfield, Conn.: Millbrook Press, 1996.

Partner, Daniel. *The House of Representatives*. Philadelphia: Chelsea House, 2000.

Phillips, Andrew. "Black, Proud and Republican," *Macleans* 110 (11 August 1997): 26.

Richardson, Gwen Daye, "Congressman J.C. Watts: GOP Rising Star." *Headway Magazine*, April 1997.

Ringle, Ken. "Carrying the GOP Ball." *Washington Post*, 4 February 1997.

Sullivan, George. *Quarterbacks: Eighteen of Football's Greatest*. New York: Atheneum BFYR, 1998.

Switzer, Barry. *Bootlegger's Boy*. New York: William Morrow, 1990.

Waldman, Amy. "The GOP's Great Black Hope." *Washington Monthly* 28 (October 1996): 34–40.

Watts, J. C. "Watts' Thoughts: OU Quarterback Shares His 1980 Season with You." *Oklahoma Sooners* 3, no. 2 (February/March 1981).

Zaslow, Jeffrey. "J. C. Watts: The Football Star-Turned-Congressman Calls for Personal Responsibility." *USA Weekend*, December 12–14, 1997.

# INDEX

# PICTURE CREDITS

NORMA JEAN LUTZ, who lives in Tulsa, Oklahoma, has been writing professionally since 1977. She is the author of more than 250 short stories and articles as well as 28 books—fiction and non-fiction. Of all the writing she does, she most enjoys writing children's books.

NATHAN IRVIN HUGGINS, one of America's leading scholars in the field of black studies, helped select the titles for the BLACK AMERICANS OF ACHIEVEMENT series, for which he also served as senior consulting editor. He was the W. E. B. DuBois Professor of History and Afro-American Studies at Harvard University and the director of the W. E. B. DuBois Institute for Afro-American Research at Harvard. He received his doctorate from Harvard in 1962 and returned there as professor in 1980 after teaching at Columbia University, the University of Massachusetts, Lake Forest College, and the California State University, Long Beach. He was the author of four books and dozens of articles, including *Black Odyssey: The Afro-American Ordeal in Slavery*, *The Harlem Renaissance*, and *Slave and Citizen: The Life of Frederick Douglass*, and was associated with the Children's Television Workshop, National Public Radio, the Boston Athenaeum, the Museum of Afro-American History, the Howard Thurman Educational Trust, and Upward Bound. Professor Huggins died in 1989, at the age of 62, in Cambridge, Massachusetts.